W9-BFP-481

Aerosmith

Hard Rock Superstars

Library Ed. ISBN-13:
978-0-7660-3031-2
Paperback ISBN-13:
978-0-7660-3623-9

Library Ed. ISBN-13:
978-0-7660-3236-1
Paperback ISBN-13:
978-1-59845-210-5

Library Ed. ISBN-13:
978-0-7660-3379-5
Paperback ISBN-13:
978-1-59845-212-9

Library Ed. ISBN-13:
978-0-7660-3232-3
Paperback ISBN-13:
978-1-59845-211-2

Library Ed. ISBN-13:
978-0-7660-3234-7
Paperback ISBN-13:
978-1-59845-208-2

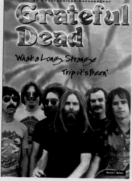

Library Ed. ISBN-13:
978-0-7660-3028-2
Paperback ISBN-13:
978-0-7660-3620-8

Library Ed. ISBN-13:
978-0-7660-3029-9
Paperback ISBN-13:
978-0-7660-3621-5

Library Ed. ISBN-13:
978-0-7660-3027-5
Paperback ISBN-13:
978-0-7660-3619-2

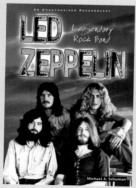

Library Ed. ISBN-13:
978-0-7660-3026-8
Paperback ISBN-13:
978-0-7660-3618-5

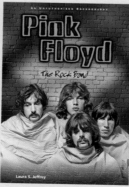

Library Ed. ISBN-13:
978-0-7660-3030-5
Paperback ISBN-13:
978-0-7660-3622-2

Library Ed. ISBN-13:
978-0-7660-3233-0
Paperback ISBN-13:
978-1-59845-213-6

Library Ed. ISBN-13:
978-0-7660-3231-6
Paperback ISBN-13:
978-1-59845-209-9

Aerosmith

Hard Rock Superstars

Jeff Burlingame

REBELS OF **ROCK**

E **Enslow Publishers, Inc.**
40 Industrial Road
Box 398
Berkeley Heights, NJ 07922
USA

http://www.enslow.com

Library of Congress Cataloging-in-Publication Data

Burlingame, Jeff.
    Aerosmith : Hard Rock Superstars / Jeff Burlingame.
        p. cm. — (Rebels of rock)
    Includes bibliographical references and index.
    Summary: "A biography of American rock band Aerosmith"—Provided by publisher.
    ISBN 978-0-7660-3236-1
    1. Aerosmith (Musical group)—Juvenile literature. 2. Rock musicians—United States—Juvenile litera-
ture. I. Title.
    ML3930.A17B87 2008
    782.42166092'2—dc22
    [B]
     2009006469

ISBN-13: 978-1-59845-210-5 (paperback ed.)

Printed in the United States of America

052010 Lake Book Manufacturing, Inc., Melrose Park, IL

10 9 8 7 6 5 4 3 2 1

To Our Readers: This book has not been authorized by Aerosmith or its successors.

We have done our best to make sure all Internet Addresses in this book were active and appropriate when we went to press. However, the author and the publisher have no control over and assume no liability for the material available on those Internet sites or on other Web sites they may link to. Any comments or suggestions can be sent by e-mail to comments@enslow.com or to the address on the back cover.

Every effort has been made to locate all copyright holders of material used in this book. If any errors or omissions have occurred, corrections will be made in future editions of this book.

♻ Enslow Publishers, Inc., is committed to printing our books on recycled paper. The paper in every book contains 10% to 30% post-consumer waste (PCW). The cover board on the outside of each book contains 100% PCW. Our goal is to do our part to help young people and the environment too!

Illustration Credits: Associated Press, pp. 6, 85; Photo by Peter Brooker/Rex USA, Courtesy Everett Collection, p. 69; Ian Dickinson/Rex Features/Courtesy Everett Collection, p. 48; Everett Collection, p. 78; Getty Images, pp. 9, 19, 54; Courtesy of Bob Gruen, p. 31; Lucas Jackson/Reuters/Landov, p. 90; Michael Ochs Archives/Getty Images, p. 43; Photofest, p. 59; © Michael Putland/Retna Ltd., pp. 12, 33; Redferns/Getty Images, pp. 22, 24, 51, 65; Time & Life Pictures/Getty Images, p. 61; WireImage, pp. 36, 80; Graham Wiltshire/Rex USA/ Courtesy Everett Collection, p. 40.

Cover Illustration: FilmMagic. Background images: Shutterstock.

CONTENTS

Aerosmith was inducted into the Rock and Roll Hall of Fame in 2001. From left to right: Joe Perry, Steven Tyler, Joey Kramer, Tom Hamilton, and Brad Whitford.

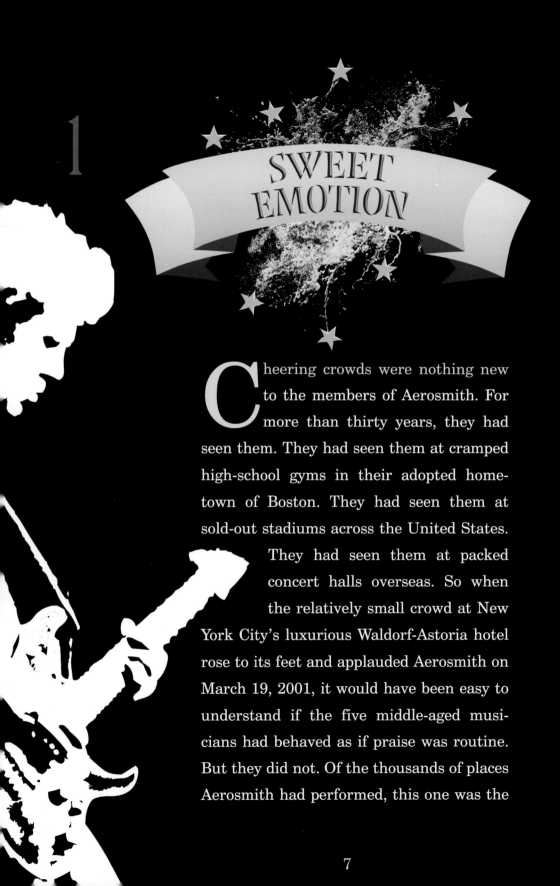

SWEET EMOTION

Cheering crowds were nothing new to the members of Aerosmith. For more than thirty years, they had seen them. They had seen them at cramped high-school gyms in their adopted home-town of Boston. They had seen them at sold-out stadiums across the United States. They had seen them at packed concert halls overseas. So when the relatively small crowd at New York City's luxurious Waldorf-Astoria hotel rose to its feet and applauded Aerosmith on March 19, 2001, it would have been easy to understand if the five middle-aged musicians had behaved as if praise was routine. But they did not. Of the thousands of places Aerosmith had performed, this one was the most special. This night, the crowd's applause was not just for another show-stopping rendition of "Walk This Way." It was not for another tear-jerking version of "Dream On." This night, the audience was applauding Aerosmith's entire career and the band's induction into the Rock and Roll Hall of Fame.

First, musician Kid Rock introduced the band as "the greatest rock band in American history."[1] Then, the five sharply dressed members of Aerosmith hit the stage to give their acceptance speeches. When bassist Tom Hamilton picked up his award, he joked: "Mom, my promise still holds. When I finally get this out of my system, I'll go to college."[2] College probably was not coming anytime soon. Even at forty-nine years old, Hamilton—and the other members of Aerosmith, three of whom were older than him—still had a lot of rock and rolling to do. And millions of fans across the world still wanted to see them do so.

Three days earlier, more than two thousand people had showed up at a New York City record store to attend a rare Aerosmith autograph session. The event was held to be perfectly timed with the release of the band's thirteenth studio album, which was the No. 2 record in the country. For more than two hours, Aerosmith signed autographs. No fan left without one. However, many people did leave with a few tears. That is because they were excited to finally have met the band they had been listening to and admiring for years.[3]

Being inducted into a hall of fame is the pinnacle of many professions. Such inductions generally come at the end of careers. But for Aerosmith it came at the beginning of yet another tour. The Rock and Roll Hall of Fame's director noticed this and said, "I think this is the first time we're inducting someone who's currently in the Top 20."[4] It was obvious. Aerosmith were still on top of their game.

Following their speeches, the same lineup that recorded the band's first album in 1973—Hamilton, singer Steven Tyler, guitarists Joe Perry and Brad Whitford, and drummer

KID ROCK (RIGHT, SINGING WITH STEVEN TYLER) PERFORMED WITH AEROSMITH DURING THEIR THE HALL OF FAME INDUCTION.

Joey Kramer—took the stage to show off the stellar musicianship and showmanship that had brought them to this moment. Kid Rock joined the band for its first song, the Aerosmith classic "Sweet Emotion." Kid Rock then left the stage and Aerosmith continued, playing the first part of their current hit, "Jaded," before segueing into "Train Kept a-Rollin'" to finish the night. A standing ovation followed.

Backstage, the band's enthusiasm and appreciation for receiving the honor continued. Tyler said, "It's totally overwhelming . . . to think that you have a room next to Elvis Presley now, is like, wow!"[5] Hamilton added his own take. He said, "I was more nervous about this than I was at the Super Bowl, *Saturday Night Live*, anything."[6]

There were several times over the course of Aerosmith's lengthy career where making the Hall of Fame seemed unlikely. In fact, there were many times where making it another day seemed impossible. That is because Aerosmith's long and winding road was paved with all the vices most people associate with the music business. There was sex. There were drugs. Somehow, after those two vices had come and gone, there still was rock 'n' roll.

COMING TOGETHER

G iven where they came from, it was unlikely the future members of Aerosmith would ever even meet. They came from different neighborhoods, different cities, and even different states. But whether it was by chance, fate, luck, or a little bit of each, the men did meet. In each instance, it was because of a common passion they shared for rock and roll.

Steven Tallarico (Steven Tyler)

Music was always a big part of Steven Victor Tallarico's life. Some might say it was in his blood. His grandfather, Giovanni, had come to America from Italy and made a living

Steven Tyler
in 1978

playing music with his brothers up and down the East Coast. Steven's grandmother, Constance, was an accomplished pianist. His father, Victor, was a classical pianist who had trained at New York City's prestigious Juilliard performing arts school. When Steven was born on March 26, 1948, in Yonkers, New York, his dad was a high-school music teacher who also gave private lessons.

Music even helped bring Steven's parents together. That happened one night when Victor Tallarico went to his girlfriend's house to pick her up. It turned out she was not home. But her best friend, Susan Blancha, was. When Tallarico heard Blancha playing piano, he asked her out instead.[1] The two proved to be a perfect match. Tallarico was in the Army, stationed at Fort Dix, New Jersey, and the couple married after World War II ended. Their first child, Lynda, was born in 1946. When Steven was born two years later, his family was living with his grandparents in Harlem, New York. Music constantly filled their middle-class home. Years later, Steven wrote, "I grew up under my father's piano. I'd sit under his big Steinway and play games and pretend things while listening to him practice for two hours every day . . . That's where I got this emotional thing I have with music."[2]

When Steven was four years old, his family moved into a sixth-floor apartment in the Bronx. It became evident early on that Steven would be a mischievous child. He was always getting into trouble. Near the end of his elementary school years,

Steven and his family moved to Yonkers. The suburban setting provided Steven with several different ways to create mischief. The kids there poked fun of the skinny Italian kid with big lips. Steven wrote that he had been beaten up by "the bad kids at the bus stop."[3] He said, "This made me hate the world more than anything else I can think of. . . . I would go home and cry about it and my mother would say, 'Don't you worry about those lips of yours, Stevie. All the better to kiss the girls with those lips.'"[4]

Each summer, Steven found peace at his family's 360-acre resort in Sunapee, New Hampshire. The resort was called Trow-Rico. There, he fished on Lake Sunapee, hunted animals, and played in the woods. Sunapee also became the site of Steven's first musical performance. He said, "All the families that came up had kids and every Friday night [Steven's aunt would] get everyone together and we would sing 'John Jacob Jingleheimer Schmidt.' She would put together little skits in the barn downstairs where she had a little stage. There was just a curtain and a few chairs in front of it. So I started there. That was the beginning of it."[5]

Steven's early skits soon morphed into playing in a band with his friend, Ray Tabano. The two boys were members of Ray's neighborhood gang, the Green Mountain Boys. Ray's dad worked in a bar and let the two teens play a few songs there when the main band was on a break. Steven played guitar and sang. Ray played drums.[6] Steven was a good drummer, too. He even played drums during several shows with his father's swing band. But the swing dance music did not do much for Steven. Its style was better suited for older folks, and not really what the long-haired fourteen-year-old wanted to be playing. He was a rebel. Rock 'n' roll music was his thing.

Steven continued his mischievous ways both in and out of school. By the time he was fifteen, he had experimented with alcohol, marijuana, and other drugs. That eventually led to him being kicked out of Roosevelt High School. He said, "[The school] told me not to come back in September. So I stole the bass drum I'd played in the marching band, [and] carried it right out of school."[7] Steven finished his formal education at an artistic private school called Quintano's School for Young Professionals.

Steven's expulsion from high school came at roughly the same time as a major shift in America's attitude toward rock 'n' roll. Throughout history, popular music often has paralleled the social and political climates of the place where it was created. In 1964, U.S. society was unsettled, due in part to the recent assassination of President John F. Kennedy. Americans also were divided over their country's involvement in a controversial war in Vietnam. Rock 'n' roll had always been a rebellious art form, and the time had come for it to undergo another major style change. Most believe that began February 7, 1964, when a plane carrying an English band named the Beatles landed at a New York airport. The Beatles' song

"I Want to Hold Your Hand" had reached number one on the U.S. music charts less than a week earlier, and American teens had fallen in love with the rebellious and brash sound played by the shaggy-haired foursome. The arrival of the Beatles marked the beginning of what was called "The British Invasion." Other British acts soon would follow the Beatles into the United States, including the Rolling Stones, the Who, and the Yardbirds.

The impact those British bands had on Steven was immense and immediate. Now sixteen, he formed his first serious rock band, and patterned it after those British bands. Steven's band was called the Strangeurs and featured Steven on drums and, for the first time, on lead vocals. The band played cover songs by the day's popular artists, including the Rolling Stones, the Byrds, the Animals, and others. The band eventually changed its name to Chain Reaction. By this time, Steven and keyboardist Don Solomon began writing their own songs and adding them to the group's repertoire. Chain Reaction played small clubs in New York and New England. They even opened for some of the day's popular performers, such as the Yardbirds and the Beach Boys, when they performed in New York.

Chain Reaction recorded two 45s, or two-sided vinyl records with a song on each side. They are called 45s because they spin on the record player at forty-five revolutions per minute. Usually one song, the A-side, is the one a band thought the radio would play and people would like most. The song on the other side is called the B-side. "The Sun" was Chain Reaction's first single, and featured "When I Needed You" as its B-side. "You Should Have Been Here Yesterday" was the band's second single, with a B-side of "Ever Lovin' Man." Not surprisingly, all the songs had a Beatles vibe. But neither of the singles brought Steven the fame he said he desired. Soon, he and Don left Chain Reaction and formed a short-lived group called William Proud.

Steven spent most of his free time hanging out in New York's Greenwich Village with people who shared similar interests, including music. The Village was known for its strong music community. Many rebellious people, like Steven, lived there and frequented the area's numerous music clubs. Greenwich Village is where Steven met the members of the band the Left Banke, which had a hit song in 1966 called "Walk Away Renee." He was impressed by the band's success. But he was not impressed with their work ethic. He said, "They had a hit under their belt, a million-seller nationwide, and they were just the laziest mothers ever."[8] He said he watched the once-successful band "flush themselves down the toilet."[9] Steven eventually sang backing vocals on a few songs on the Left Banke's 1968 album, *The Left Banke Too*.

Steven Tallarico later wrote that the biggest highlight of the time he spent in Greenwich Village came in 1965, when he attended a Rolling Stones concert. He said, "Everybody told me that I looked just like [Rolling Stones singer] Mick Jagger with my big lips, and [Rolling Stones guitarist] Keith Richards basically was the music I used to love more than anything."[10] A photograph in Aerosmith's 1997 autobiography, *Walk This Way*, shows Tallarico standing behind Jagger outside a hotel. Tallarico wrote that he and his friends "hung around for a while, buzzing like crazy just because we got to touch them!"[11]

Yet even in New York City, Tallarico still could not find the musical stardom he sought. So, in the summer of 1969, he hitchhiked north to his family's place in Sunapee. Far from the big city of New York, small-town Sunapee seemed like an unlikely place for Tallarico to find what he was looking for. But he did.

Joe Perry

Born September 10, 1950, in Lawrence, Massachusetts, Anthony Joseph "Joe" Perry's background paralleled Tallarico's. Joe also came from a middle-class, musical family. Joe's family wanted him to train in classical music. But Joe, like Tallarico, had been deeply influenced by the Beatles, the Rolling Stones, and other British Invasion groups. Rock 'n' roll was Joe's thing.

Joe grew up in the small Massachusetts town of Hopedale. His father, Anthony, was an accountant and had served in the Army. His mother, Mary, was a teacher. He had one sister,

Joe Perry
in the
early 1970s

Anne. Joe received his first guitar when he was nine and joined his first band when he was fourteen. That was in 1964, the same year the Beatles made their historic first visit to the United States. He said he and his band members would go around "pretending we were the Beatles. We'd sing [Bob] Dylan songs and Byrds' songs and one time we actually played at a party and sang in the corner. . . . [I]t wasn't very good."[12]

Despite having well-educated parents, Joe never was a good student. He dropped out of high school, and his parents sent him to a prep school in Saxtons River, Vermont. There, he joined a band called Just Us, and also played in a band called Flash. Music—mostly playing guitar—was Joe's main focus. As it was for Tallarico, school was a distant second, or even third, priority. Joe later said, "As far back as I can remember, it was a struggle being in school. . . . I just wasn't a good fit."[13] Joe's parents eventually sent him to a private school called Vermont Academy, and he stayed there until he almost graduated—before dropping out. While at the school, he performed in a couple of rock bands.

Perry eventually wound up in Sunapee, where his family—like Tallarico's—owned property. He worked a few part-time jobs in Sunapee, including one as a dishwasher at The Anchorage ice-cream parlor. It was there he met a tall, blonde kid named Tom Hamilton who soon would help him take his musical career to the next level.

Tom Hamilton

Thomas William Hamilton was born December 31, 1951, in Colorado Springs, Colorado. His father was an Air Force colonel, so his family moved a lot. Tom's father eventually left the Air Force, and the Hamilton family moved just east of Sunapee Lake to New London, New Hampshire.

Like Tallarico and Perry, Hamilton was heavily into music—both listening to it and playing it. Hamilton's instrument of choice was the bass guitar. He and guitarist Perry soon teamed up and played in a few bands together, including one they called Jam Band.

Perry met another person at The Anchorage who would be vital to his musical career: Tallarico. Perry said, "I knew who he was. Everybody in Sunapee did . . . Steven would come in with his bands and they'd act like they figured rock stars are supposed to, throwing food, real loud and obnoxious . . . this little town that looked up to them as the local rock stars."[14] In the summer of 1970, he invited Tallarico to watch Jam Band play at a local hot spot called The Barn. Tallarico did, and was impressed. He soon joined forces with Perry and Hamilton. Tallarico's bandmate from William Proud, Ray Tabano, was brought in to play rhythm guitar.

Ray Tabano

Raymond Tabano was born December 23, 1946, in the Bronx, New York. He and Tallarico met as youngsters and were

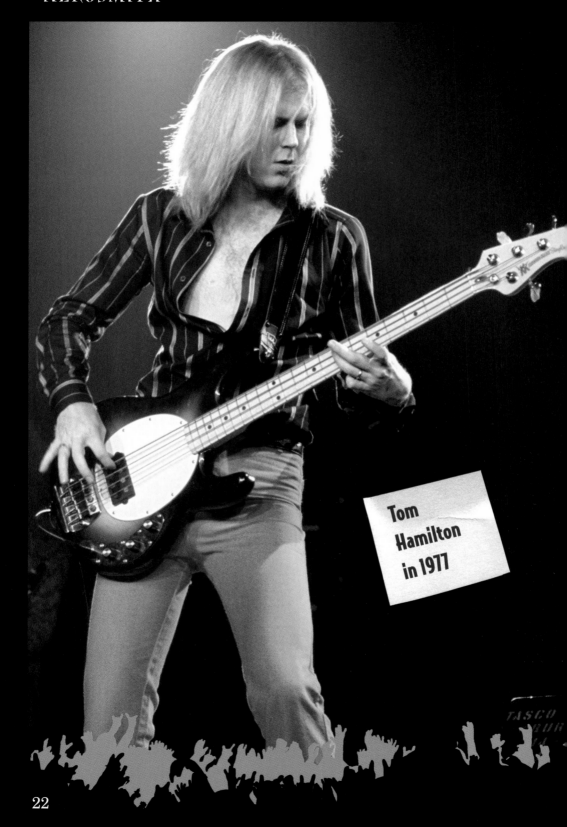

Tom
Hamilton
in 1977

good friends throughout their days at Roosevelt High School. When he was invited to play guitar with Tallarico, Perry, and Hamilton in 1970, Tabano was living in Boston, Massachusetts, operating a leather goods store there. So he suggested the foursome make Boston their home base. They all agreed.

Initially, Tallarico played drums and sang in the new group. But what he really wanted was to be the lead singer, out in the front of the stage showing off his energetic persona. He wanted to jump around and excite the crowd. He wanted to be the star. To allow him to do this, the foursome needed to find a drummer. They found him in Boston. Joey Kramer was the final piece of the new band's puzzle.

Joey Kramer

Joseph Michael Kramer was born June 21, 1950, in the Bronx, New York. He was the oldest of four children. When he was young, his family moved to Yonkers, where he eventually attended Roosevelt High School with Tallarico and Tabano. Like those two, Kramer also had played in many different bands. When his high-school friends began their search for a drummer for their unnamed new band, Kramer was immediately interested. He happened to be in Boston at the time, studying at the prestigious Berklee College of Music. Kramer auditioned and won the drumming gig. The still-unnamed band's lineup was solidified. Kramer did more than just fill

Joey Kramer in 1976

the drummer's role. He also gave the group its name. He said, "A girl I went to high school with and I used to write it all over our books because I knew that someday I was going to be in a band and that it was going to be named that!"[15]

The name was Aerosmith. Many people believe the name was just a misspelling of the title of a popular Sinclair Lewis novel, *Arrowsmith*. In truth, it has no meaning.

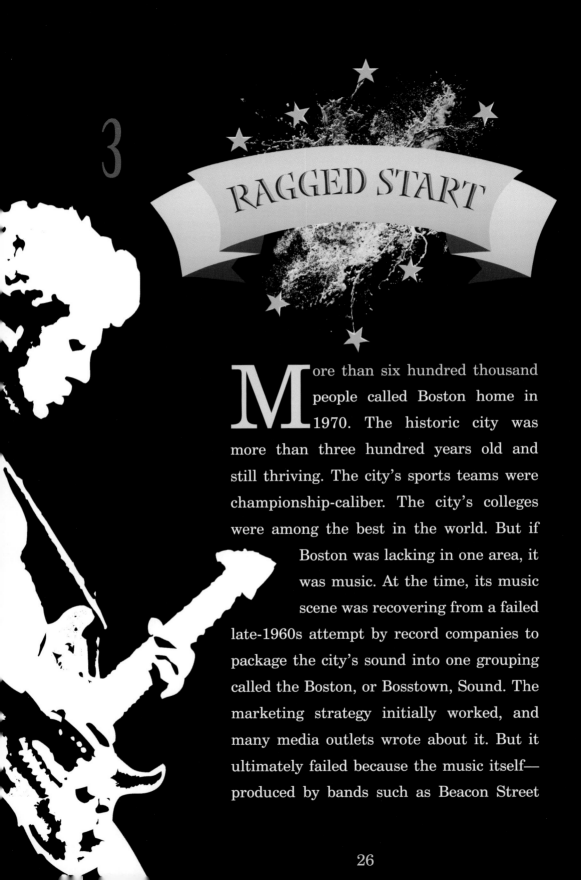

3

RAGGED START

More than six hundred thousand people called Boston home in 1970. The historic city was more than three hundred years old and still thriving. The city's sports teams were championship-caliber. The city's colleges were among the best in the world. But if Boston was lacking in one area, it was music. At the time, its music scene was recovering from a failed late-1960s attempt by record companies to package the city's sound into one grouping called the Boston, or Bosstown, Sound. The marketing strategy initially worked, and many media outlets wrote about it. But it ultimately failed because the music itself—produced by bands such as Beacon Street

Union, Orpheus, and Ultimate Spinach—failed to keep the public's attention.

So when the members of Aerosmith came to town in 1970, Boston's music scene was not very well respected. In fact, Boston barely had an original music scene. The city was filled with cover bands playing small bars and clubs. Successful original bands hardly existed. Best-known among the Boston bands was the J. Geils Band, which had released its first album on Atlantic Records the same year Aerosmith came to town. The J. Geils Band went on to become one of the most popular acts of the 1970s, and soon was selling out arenas across the country. Over the years, the J. Geils Band had a string of hit singles, including 1982's "Centerfold," which reached number one on the pop music charts the year of its release. But outside of the J. Geils Band, there was little else in Boston in 1970.

The setting of Aerosmith's first concert was nowhere near as glamorous as the arenas the J. Geils Band would soon be selling out. In fact, Aerosmith's first venue was about as far removed from an arena as a band could get. It was the gymnasium of Nipmuc Regional High School in Mendon, Massachusetts. But those who were there in the fall of 1970 still experienced something special. Prior to the show, Tallarico stole one of the school's T-shirts from a locker. A photo of the band taken during the performance shows him wearing it on stage. Those who were there did not seem to care about

Tallarico's petty thievery. To hear them talk now, all they noticed was the band's enormous talent.

Student Roy Spindel was among the crowd of about one hundred fifty people. Now a counselor at the school, Spindel said he was pleased with Aerosmith's set. He said, "I remember being blown away by their sound. When they were playing, it seemed obvious they were going to go someplace. All I could think of was, 'This is what it must feel like when the Rolling Stones play.' They sounded like they had been together forever."[1] Aerosmith played songs by the Beatles, the Rolling Stones, and others. They also played a solid selection of originals. The crowd seemed to enjoy both, especially the high energy level at which the group performed. Energetic performances like the one at Nipmuc would help Aerosmith build—and maintain for four decades—a reputation as a great live band.

Another unfortunate pattern began the night of Aerosmith's first show. It was the band members arguing with one another, especially Tallarico and Perry. At the Nipmuc show, the two argued over the volume of Perry's guitar. Tallarico thought it was too loud. Perry said it needed to be that loud to achieve the sound he wanted. He said, "I'm doing my thing, and to do it I have to be loud."[2] Within the band, Tallarico had the reputation of being a perfectionist. Throughout the years, he and other band members often argued because of it.

Life at Home

If Aerosmith's first live show was unglamorous, the lives of the five band members were even more so. The five young men shared a three-bedroom apartment on Commonwealth Avenue in Boston. Rent on the less-than-perfect pad was paid by part-time jobs. Tallarico worked in a bakery. Perry worked in a synagogue, a Jewish house of worship. Times were tough, but the five musicians were determined to do what it took to continue their music careers. Tallarico told one magazine, "[S]ome of us were living in the kitchen, eating brown rice and Campbell's soup. Those days, you know, when a quart of beer was heaven. It was hard times and it was really good."[3]

The band lived near the campus of Boston University. Their location was beneficial in many ways. Tallarico said, "We managed to get a free practice room at a Boston University dorm by promising to play some dances for them. . . . They were really nice. They'd even sneak us some free meals at the cafeteria when we were hard up for food."[4] The school—and its students—also fit nicely into Aerosmith's plans for playing live. They did not want to play the types of clubs many bands did, places that wanted them to play other people's music. They wanted to play venues where they could play their own songs. In general, younger audiences such as those students at Boston University are more accepting of newer music and not necessarily only interested in hearing bands play the day's hit songs. So the members of Aerosmith often would

spontaneously set up their equipment outside the school and perform to whatever crowd might gather. They would do the same at various high schools, bars, private parties, and other places that would have them. The goal was to perform and get noticed, hopefully by someone with connections that could take them to the top. They made great strides in doing so. They also had countless setbacks.

Their first big setback involved guitarist Ray Tabano. Tallarico's longtime friend was not getting along with the rest of the band. Soon, he was out. The reasons for his departure vary. Most stories say Tallarico wanted to keep Tabano in the band, but the other members felt he was not good enough and did not fit in. They wanted to fire him. Tabano himself said, "I knew those guys were a lot better than me, music-wise. I was struggling and fighting to survive and Tom would tell me, 'You really don't play that good, man,' and I'd want to murder him."[5] Tabano eventually returned to the Aerosmith team and became the band's director of marketing. He helped design the band's popular winged logo.

With Tabano out, Aerosmith needed a new guitarist. In the summer of 1971, they found one. Brad Whitford was only nineteen, but was an experienced musician when Aerosmith approached him about filling their vacancy. The band he left behind, Justin Tyme, was popular in Boston, but Whitford quickly made up his mind that Aerosmith was the band he should be in. Years later, he said, "I listened to them for about ten minutes and thought to myself, '*I should probably do this*.'"[6] Ironically, Tabano later took Whitford's guitar spot in Justin Tyme.

Brad Whitford

Bradley Earnest Whitford brought a mountain of musical experience to Aerosmith. Born February 23, 1952, in Winchester, Massachusetts, Whitford had been a musician for several years. His mother was a housewife and his father was a systems analyst. At a young age, Whitford began playing the

AEROSMITH IN 1973

trumpet. He played the trumpet for three years until age fourteen, when he discovered his true musical passion, the guitar. He honed that guitar playing with several local bands. After graduating high school in 1970, Whitford—like Joey Kramer—ended up in Boston at Berklee College of Music.

After Whitford agreed to join Aerosmith, he immediately moved into the band's Boston apartment. What he saw inside the brick building shocked him. Band members and their friends were using drugs and drinking alcohol. Women were coming and going from the apartment. The quarters were cramped. At first, Whitford did not even have a bed. He had to sleep on the couch in the living room. The band eventually wrote a song about the experience of living on Commonwealth. It was called "Movin' Out," and would show up on Aerosmith's first album.

Whitford's first show as a member of Aerosmith was in August 1971, at a club called The Savage Beast in Brownsville, Vermont. He had dozens of shows under his belt by December, when Aerosmith played its biggest show to date at the Academy of Music in New York City. Aerosmith was the opening act on the bill with Humble Pie and Edgar Winter's band. The theater's marquee afforded the band little respect, listing their name as two separate words, "Aero Smith," instead of one.

Opening for more-popular acts is difficult to do. The crowd is there to see the main acts, and often does not pay

Brad Whitford in the late 1970s

much attention to the openers. Oftentimes, the opening acts are almost totally ignored. If they want attention, or anyone to even listen, they often have to work hard for it. So the pressure was on Aerosmith to try and win the crowd over. And they did. The band was only scheduled to play three songs, but kept going after the third one. The audience did not seem to mind. In fact, they enjoyed it. Hamilton said, "I was surprised how much the audience liked us. There was a lot of applause."[7]

A Record Deal

Aerosmith's permanent lineup was intact and getting better with each show. Money was not exactly rolling in, but opportunities were. John O'Toole gave one big one to the band. O'Toole managed Boston's Fenway Theatre and allowed the band to practice there for free. He also quickly became an Aerosmith fan. One day, O'Toole told music promoter Frank Connelly that he should come see them play. Connelly—who band members soon called "Father Frank" because he was like a parent to them—liked what he saw when he did. He began to help Aerosmith in several areas. First, he booked them rooms in the Manchester Sheraton Hotel. The band lived and practiced there. Then, Connelly helped the band strike a business deal with Steve Leber and David Krebs, a management team from New York. The Leber-Krebs team helped Aerosmith become a lot more professional. The duo set up a showcase, or music industry audition, for the band at Max's Kansas City club in New York City. The audition was successful. After the show, Clive Davis, president of Columbia Records, told the band he was impressed. He said, "Yes, I think we could do something with you."[8]

Davis held true to his word. In the summer of 1972, Aerosmith signed a $125,000 contract with Columbia Records. At the time, it was an enormous amount of money for a band to receive. The days of struggling to find enough cash to pay the rent and buy food appeared to be over. But more challenges were ahead.

Aerosmith recorded its first album in 1973.

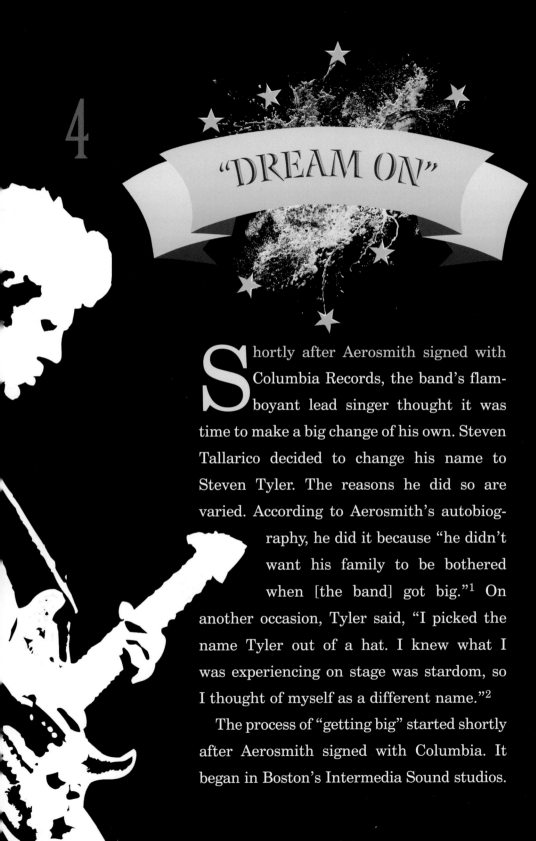

4

"DREAM ON"

Shortly after Aerosmith signed with Columbia Records, the band's flamboyant lead singer thought it was time to make a big change of his own. Steven Tallarico decided to change his name to Steven Tyler. The reasons he did so are varied. According to Aerosmith's autobiography, he did it because "he didn't want his family to be bothered when [the band] got big."[1] On another occasion, Tyler said, "I picked the name Tyler out of a hat. I knew what I was experiencing on stage was stardom, so I thought of myself as a different name."[2]

The process of "getting big" started shortly after Aerosmith signed with Columbia. It began in Boston's Intermedia Sound studios.

That is where the band went to record its first album. The studio's equipment was old, but the band had polished its sound during its numerous live performances and practices. No high-tech studio trickery was necessary to make Aerosmith sound good. Primitive equipment would do. And primitive it was. Whitford said the studio had a "recording console that was literally homemade. Part of it was cardboard with knobs the size of headlights."[3]

After just two weeks in the studio with producer Adrian Barber, the band had completed recording its first album. It was simply titled *Aerosmith*. The eight-song album was released in early 1973. It began with "Make It," a song about aspiring to become a star. The album's highlights included "Mama Kin," a bluesy rock song that Tyler enjoyed so much he had the words "Ma Kin" tattooed on his left arm. Despite Tyler's enthusiasm for "Mama Kin," the album's standout track was the third song, "Dream On." Tyler had written the song when he was seventeen, using his father's piano. Some of Aerosmith's members—including Perry—did not think much of it, mostly because it was a slow ballad. Perry was more into faster-paced songs. Today, "Dream On" is widely believed to have been the first power ballad, or rock song that begins slowly and later builds to a faster, more powerful pace. "Dream On" is about "the hunger [and] desire and ambition to be somebody that Aerosmith felt in those days."[4]

"Dream On" helped fill that hunger. It became a hit on

radio stations in the band's hometown of Boston. Columbia Records eventually released the song as a single. It peaked at number fifty-nine on the *Billboard* singles charts. It was a decent showing, but the impact it made nationally was minimal. Tyler had been convinced the song would be the key to obtaining widespread success. It did not work that way, at least not yet.

Hearing from the Critics

As for the whole album, a few critics enjoyed it. One magazine writer said, "I like this band because they seem to know themselves; there's . . . just a full LP [long-play album] of screaming, metallic, creative rock and roll."[5]

But many critics did not like Aerosmith—the band or the album. To them, the band was nothing more than the American version of the Rolling Stones: Tyler was Mick Jagger and Perry was Keith Richards. Physically, the men did resemble each other. People often told Tyler he looked like Jagger, and Tyler said he was flattered with the comparison. Tyler idolized Jagger. He and the rest of the band were flattered every time they were told Aerosmith's music sounded similar to the Rolling Stones. In many ways, it did. But it also sounded similar to Led Zeppelin, the Byrds, the Beatles, and many other groups that had influenced the members of Aerosmith.

Just as Aerosmith's career momentum was growing, the band suffered a huge setback. The man that had signed

AEROSMITH'S STEVEN TYLER
AND JOE PERRY WERE OFTEN
COMPARED TO THE ROLLING
STONES'S MICK JAGGER
(LEFT) AND KEITH RICHARDS
(RIGHT).

Aerosmith to its record deal, Clive Davis, was fired from Columbia Records over a financial scandal. Aerosmith's top supporter was gone. After that, the band received little support from the label.

In March and April 1973, Aerosmith played several shows in and around Boston, no doubt spurred by the radio success of "Dream On," and a couple of shows opening for the Kinks, another of the British Invasion bands that had made a large splash in America. In the fall, Aerosmith left on a cross-country tour opening for Mott the Hoople, who had a hit song called "All the Young Dudes."

They played colleges, coliseums, and everywhere in between. On December 15, Aerosmith struck TV gold when they were invited to play "Dream On" on a popular show called *American Bandstand*. It was the band's national television debut. Years later, host Dick Clark still remembered the band's performance on his show. He said,

"I felt then that Steven and the rest of the guys had a special quality that would enable them to hang around for a long time."[6]

Follow-up Time

The pressure was on when Aerosmith entered New York City's Record Plant studio in the fall of 1973 to record its second album. The band's first record had sold tens of thousands of copies. It was a high number for a new band, but nowhere near the amount Columbia had hoped to sell. So producers Ray Colcord and Jack Douglas were brought in to record the album. Douglas—who had worked with Beatle John Lennon on his second solo album, *Imagine*—and Aerosmith quickly hit it off. Whitford later said Douglas was "like our sixth member. We did everything together. In the studio he was open to anything, always willing to experiment."[7] Douglas also worked the band members hard in the studio. What they came out with was *Get Your Wings*, an eight-song album that captured the energy and the sleazy attitude of Aerosmith's live performances far better than their first album had. The record kicked off with the first single, "Same Old Song and Dance." The song was to become a radio favorite for years to come. Perhaps more importantly, the song showcased for the first time what the songwriting team of Tyler and Perry could accomplish. The Rolling Stones had their star singer/guitarist duo in Jagger and Richards. Led Zeppelin had theirs in Robert

Plant and Jimmy Page. Now Aerosmith had theirs in Tyler and Perry.

Get Your Wings also included Aerosmith's cover of the classic blues song, "Train Kept A-Rollin'." The Yardbirds had covered the song nearly a decade earlier, and Aerosmith frequently performed the song live in concert. In fact, Aerosmith wanted to record "Train Kept A-Rollin'" live for their new album, but it was too inconvenient to do so. So Douglas made the song sound live by using some studio trickery. To this day, many people still believe the version of the song on *Get Your Wings* was recorded live.

Get Your Wings was released in March 1974 to basically the same public reaction as Aerosmith's first album. It sold well in the Boston area and the rest of the Northeast, where the band was highly popular. Several reviewers also gave the album high marks. But Tyler said many reviewers would spend as much time focusing on his flamboyant wardrobe as they would on his band's music. Tyler's style of dress certainly gathered its share of attention. He described his wardrobe in Aerosmith's autobiography: "[T]he scarves, ragged sleeves, streamers, laces, open shirts . . . the rags developed out of poverty. I couldn't afford stuff and so my girlfriend at the time started making things for me on her sewing machine."[8]

Get Your Wings barely made a splash outside the Northeast. To remedy this, Aerosmith again hit the road, hoping to sell

IN 1974, AEROSMITH RELEASED *GET YOUR WINGS*. THE ALBUM DID WELL IN THE NORTHEAST, BUT THE BAND WANTED MORE WIDESPREAD SUCCESS.

themselves to others. Again, they played with many of the day's more popular acts, including Uriah Heep, Blue Öyster Cult, and Queen. The touring eventually paid off. By early 1975, *Get Your Wings* had sold more than five hundred thousand copies, making it Aerosmith's first gold record. The same year, Aerosmith's self-titled debut album also went gold.

Aerosmith's music was finally selling well. But the band members were not doing well personally. Drinking was a daily occurrence—and drug use was, too. Tyler said, "[T]hose were the days when I had to do as much [drugs] as I could to keep that buzz going every waking minute of the day. I had to be in that buzz. . . . I wanted it all the time or I'd be jumping out of my skin. Wherever we went, we brought the party with us."[9]

Third Time's a Charm?

In early 1975, Aerosmith and Douglas went back to the Record Plant and began working on album number three. The constant live performances had made the band members better musicians, and it showed in the studio this time around. When *Toys in the Attic* was released in April, the buying public took a liking to the band's more mature sound. Perry's bluesy guitar riffs on songs like "Toys in the Attic," "Sweet Emotion," and "Walk This Way" were tremendously catchy. Tyler's lyrics were full of humor, as well as references to sex and decadence, everything rock 'n' roll was supposed to be about. The songs were raw, yet polished—rough, yet smooth. The band's influences, such as the Rolling Stones, the Yardbirds, and Led Zeppelin, still were there. But now they were subtler. Aerosmith had separated itself from its idols, and established its own sound.

Aerosmith's incessant touring helped album sales soar. So did the popularity of "Walk This Way" and "Last Child." Both songs cracked *Billboard*'s Top 40. The sexually themed "Walk This Way" became a huge radio hit and still is considered one of the band's best songs.

Even in their hometown of Boston, the quintet always had to open for larger acts when they played in big venues.

However, when *Toys in the Attic* was released, this no longer was the case. When the tour landed at the Boston Garden for back-to-back shows, Aerosmith was the headliner. By the end of 1975, Aerosmith was the top-selling artist at Columbia Records.[10] Soon, Aerosmith would be the headliner anywhere they played in the United States.

The success of Aerosmith's current album helped sell the band's early material. Columbia Records rereleased "Dream On" at the beginning of 1976. The power ballad found its way back onto *Billboard*'s charts. It reached number six, making it Aerosmith's first Top Ten song. When "Dream On" fell from the Top 40 nearly three months later, Aerosmith scored again. This time it was with a nine-song album of hard-hitting tracks, *Rocks*. Kicking off with what was to become a classic, "Back in the Saddle," and ending with the ballad "Home Tonight," *Rocks* is considered by many critics and fans to be Aerosmith's finest hour. Some might argue that statement, but no one could debate that *Rocks* was the band's best-selling album to date. Despite only one single, "Back in the Saddle," reaching the Top 40, *Rocks* went platinum, or sold one million copies, shortly after its May release.

The pattern of constant touring began again after *Rocks* was released. Aerosmith was the headliner everywhere this time. The tour kicked off at the eighty-thousand-seat Silverdome in Pontiac, Michigan. It sold out. Other venues— including New York's Madison Square Garden, Pittsburgh's

Three Rivers Stadium, and Chicago's Comiskey Park—sold out, too.

Unfortunately, problems in the band members' personal lives were growing, as well. Tyler said the constant touring played a role in how the band members behaved when they were off the road. He said, "In the early days we were seen as a cash cow. We were worked to death. We did three shows a week and we were kept on [cocaine]. No one ever once said, 'You guys had better take a break.'. . . It was tour-album-tour-album-tour-album. There were no breaks."[11]

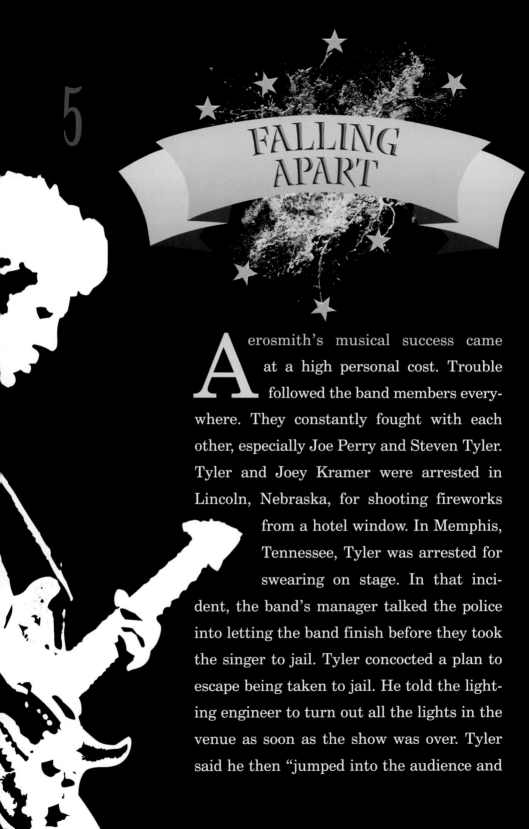

FALLING APART

5

Aerosmith's musical success came at a high personal cost. Trouble followed the band members everywhere. They constantly fought with each other, especially Joe Perry and Steven Tyler. Tyler and Joey Kramer were arrested in Lincoln, Nebraska, for shooting fireworks from a hotel window. In Memphis, Tennessee, Tyler was arrested for swearing on stage. In that incident, the band's manager talked the police into letting the band finish before they took the singer to jail. Tyler concocted a plan to escape being taken to jail. He told the lighting engineer to turn out all the lights in the venue as soon as the show was over. Tyler said he then "jumped into the audience and

Aerosmith was at its peak when the band started to fall apart. Tension was high between Steven Tyler and Joe Perry.

ran up the aisle. But just as I reached the lobby, police surrounded me with guns drawn, shouting, 'Hold it!' They handcuffed me."[1]

Exhaustion and stress caused some of the band's problems. But most of Aerosmith's woes were due to drug use. Band members had long drunk alcohol, smoked marijuana, and popped pills. But as their income increased, so did the use of harder, more expensive drugs, such as cocaine and heroin. Tyler and Perry were using these regularly by the mid-1970s. The drug use would soon catch up to the band. But for now, the members kept the machine going.

In October 1976, the five members of Aerosmith left on their first European tour. There, they played smaller concert halls in England, Scotland, Germany, and France. The tour was close to being a complete failure. People were hesitant to come out to the shows, in part because the media was particularly harsh on the band. One paper even said the outlandishly dressed Tyler looked like a girl.[2] Financially, the tour lost a lot of money. So did a short tour of Japan at the beginning of 1977. Tom Hamilton said the band members were highly intoxicated when they landed in the country and had a hard time finding their way around.[3] It obviously was not a good beginning to their trip. The rest of the visit did not go so well, either. Some of the Japanese shows had to be canceled due to the band's reckless behavior. However, band members said the fans that did attend shows were enthusiastic. Hamilton said,

"We'd leave the halls and it seemed like half the audience was waiting for us at the stage door. We could only stare out the car windows as the kids chased us for blocks."[4]

Home Sweet Home?

Back in the United States, Aerosmith was more popular than ever. Radio stations across the country had the band's songs on regular rotation. But the band members were burned out. So they took a few months off from touring and recording. The goal was for the band members to rest. But the idle time turned out to be just more time for them to drink, use drugs, and partake of other kinds of debauchery.

When the band was finally ready to record the follow-up to the smash hit *Rocks*, they did not return to the Record Plant in New York City. Instead, the band and producer Jack Douglas went to a three-hundred-room convent, the Cenacle, in the small town of Armonk, New York. The goal was to keep the band as isolated as possible from the negative temptations the Big Apple had to offer. It was David Krebs's plan, and it basically worked for Hamilton, Kramer, and Whitford. They showed up for practice every day, ready to record. But Perry and Tyler often went missing. Whitford said, "Steven and Joe just weren't around. They were locked away in their rooms consuming whatever they were consuming. We were still functioning. We still got up in the morning. So Tom, Joey, and I had a lot of time together."[5] Perry added,

"We saw it as sort of a vacation. So we went off and rented this nunnery and it was just total party time."[6]

Perry and Tyler eventually did make their way to the studio long enough to put their parts together for the album. But by that point, the studio costs were way over budget. Released just before Christmas 1977, *Draw the Line* was a solid effort, though nowhere near the quality of Aerosmith's previous two albums. None of the album's singles cracked the Top 40, though the album's fierce opener, "Draw the Line," came close to doing so. The album featured Perry's debut as lead vocalist on the amped-up song, "Bright Light Fright." The song itself

AEROSMITH PERFORMED IN THE UNITED KINGDOM IN 1976.

did not make a splash, but it did set the stage for a future endeavor Perry would soon take. *Rolling Stone* magazine called *Draw the Line* "a truly horrendous record. . . . Aerosmith sounds like a band just starting out—very much, in fact, like amateurs."[7]

Producer Douglas explained why he thought *Draw the Line* was not as good as Aerosmith's previous two smash albums: "Heroin is what did it. They came in [to the studio] with no songs, which was nothing new. They'd bring seedlings of music and we'd make that into songs. But I couldn't get them all in the same room anymore. Joe and Steven were smacked out and [Hamilton, Kramer and Whitford] were coke-crazy. All day they'd be doing anything but music, shooting guns, getting high, whatever."[8] During that time, Kramer and Perry were both involved in high-speed car wrecks. Kramer smashed his Ferrari into a guardrail and had to have several stitches. Perry also hit a guardrail in his Corvette. It soon became clear to all: the band was falling apart.

Aerosmith's loyal fans, however, still bought *Draw the Line*. They bought enough that it went platinum and hit number eleven on the *Billboard* charts. Aerosmith left on another stadium tour to promote the album. With band members squabbling more and more, the tour was a mixed success. Highlights included a headlining spot at the California Jam II music festival at the Ontario Speedway in Ontario, California. Heart, Santana, Ted Nugent, and several other bands helped draw 350,000 people to the event. It was the band's biggest stage yet, but Aerosmith did not rise to the challenge and performed a lackluster set.

In an effort to get back to their roots, Aerosmith played a couple of small club dates between stadium shows. The band billed itself as Dr. J. Jones and the Interns. It did not matter what the band called itself. The clubs still sold out.

Movie Stars

In the middle of 1978, a non-musical venture beckoned. The members of Aerosmith appeared in the movie *Sgt. Peppers Lonely Hearts Club Band*. The film was loosely based on the Beatles album of the same name. In the film, the five members of Aerosmith played a band of bad guys called the Future Villain Band. Most critics who saw the movie panned it. One said, "The musical numbers are strung together so mindlessly that the movie has the feel of an interminable variety show. Characters are named, invented or introduced to one another simply to provide excuses for the various songs."[9] The plot of the movie was even changed at Tyler's insistence. The original script had him killed off by musician Peter Frampton. But Tyler and the rest of the band did not like that. They thought it would be bad for Tyler's image. The scene was changed, and Tyler was instead pushed to his death by another character.

Being involved in the film project, which also featured Frampton as well as the Bee Gees, was not an entirely bad

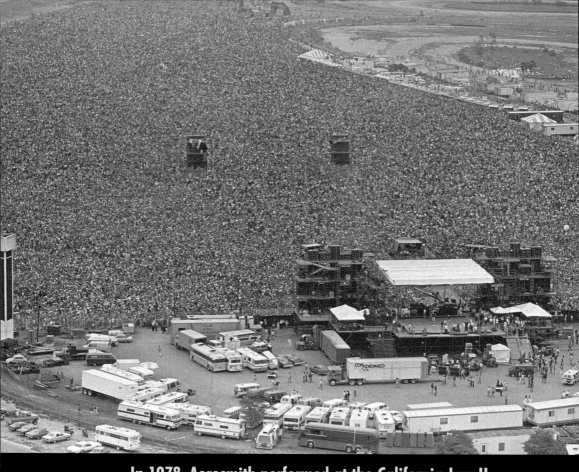

In 1978, Aerosmith performed at the California Jam II.

experience. The film's sound track included Aerosmith's version of the Beatles' hit, "Come Together." Aerosmith's version peaked at number twenty-seven on the *Billboard* singles chart, higher than any song from Aerosmith's most recent studio album. As it turns out, it would be the last time Aerosmith's name appeared on the charts for nearly ten years. The band was doing anything but coming together. Hamilton said, "We started hearing the rumors that we were breaking up when word got out how crazy things were. We'd gotten to a very dangerous point where we could afford all the vices we wanted. We had our mansions, our Ferraris, the bottomless [drug] stashes. Where do you go from there?"[10]

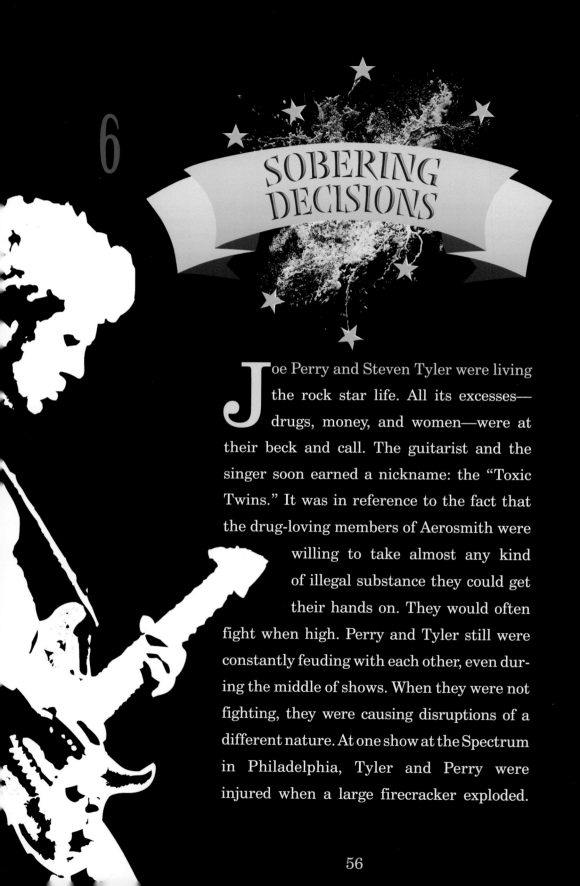

SOBERING DECISIONS

Joe Perry and Steven Tyler were living the rock star life. All its excesses—drugs, money, and women—were at their beck and call. The guitarist and the singer soon earned a nickname: the "Toxic Twins." It was in reference to the fact that the drug-loving members of Aerosmith were willing to take almost any kind of illegal substance they could get their hands on. They would often fight when high. Perry and Tyler still were constantly feuding with each other, even during the middle of shows. When they were not fighting, they were causing disruptions of a different nature. At one show at the Spectrum in Philadelphia, Tyler and Perry were injured when a large firecracker exploded.

Guitarist Brad Whitford remembered, "Steven's holding his eyes and yelling that he can't see. Joe Perry's right hand is spurting blood. Steven and Joe got a police escort to the hospital."[1] Tyler's cornea was burned and he had to wear an eye patch. The rest of that month's concerts were canceled.

Both of the Toxic Twins were married by this point. Perry was married to his longtime girlfriend, Elyssa. Tyler had just married Cyrinda Foxe, a well-known party girl and ex-wife of David Johansen, singer for the New York Dolls. Johansen later became an actor. Foxe herself was an actress and had left Johansen for Tyler. The Toxic Twins' wives soon began to feud with each other nearly as much as their superstar husbands did. Elyssa Perry said she believed Cyrinda had used her just to get together with Tyler.[2] Cyrinda said, "She had been my best friend until I started seeing Steven, and then she went ballistic."[3] Aerosmith's lead singer was fighting with its star guitarist. The wives of the two men also were fighting. Creating quality music—or simply surviving—in such a hostile environment was nearly impossible.

That the band was able to exist at all in this climate is amazing. That they were able to occasionally thrive was nearly a miracle. The band's entourage was gigantic—and costly. Members traveled from show to show in a Lear jet, rather than by bus. The release of a live album, *Live! Bootleg*, in late 1978, helped the band keep its momentum. Little studio work was done on the album, which made it sound as close to a live performance as possible. Fans loved it and the album quickly went platinum. Band members often have said they released the album because they were frustrated with the number of unofficial, or "bootleg," albums of their live material that were in circulation.

The feuding members soon headed back into the studio to record their sixth album. But they were not happy to be back. Longtime producer Jack Douglas, once called the band's "sixth member," was fired and replaced by Gary Lyons before the recording sessions, which were held in Manhattan's Mediasound Studios. Perry and Tyler were fighting more than ever. In fact, each refused to be in the studio at the same time as the other. Perry recorded his guitar tracks when Tyler was away. Tyler, on the other hand, did not visit the studio often. When he was there, he was not in any condition to write or sing lyrics. The recording process took so long that the band's record label began losing a lot of money. So Aerosmith was sent back out on tour to make some of the money back. Despite their internal troubles, Aerosmith still was able to sell out stadiums across the United States, and with that ability came a lot of money. Around the same time, the band's management gave Perry a room service bill for $80,000. He now owed management $100,000. He was given an option: if he would record a solo album, his debt would be forgiven. In light of his large debt, Perry reluctantly agreed to do so.

GUITARIST JIMMY CRESPO (FAR RIGHT) REPLACED JOE
PERRY IN AEROSMITH FROM 1979–1984.

Separate Ways

As might be expected, Perry's move to solo work further angered Tyler. Backstage at a show in Cleveland, the fighting between Tyler and Perry came to a head. The two men began arguing and then the wives of the band members joined in. When Elyssa Perry threw milk on Tom Hamilton's wife, Terry, Joe Perry decided he had had enough. He wanted out of the band. Tyler said, "The drugs won. We split up over a glass of spilt milk. . . . All the pressures of the last 10 years, all the violence came out like a pressure hole exploding."[4]

Aerosmith finished the album, *Night in the Ruts*, without Perry. Released in late 1979, *Night in the Ruts* kicked off with a decent Tyler-Perry collaboration called "No Surprize." The album also included a song called "Mia," which Tyler had written about his young daughter, born three days before Christmas in 1978. *Night in the Ruts* sold reasonably well, yet did not have any Top 40 singles. The tour featured twenty-four-year-old New Yorker Jimmy Crespo filling in for Perry on guitar. Crespo's first tour with the band did not last long, though it had nothing to do with his performance. A few shows into the tour, Tyler collapsed onstage during a performance. The rest of the tour was canceled. That incident marked the beginning of a very bad period for the lead singer.

Meanwhile, the Joe Perry Project was taking off. The group released its first album in early 1980. The album's title, *Let the Music Do the Talking*, was a direct stab at the feuding Perry had experienced during his time in Aerosmith. The album's first song was also called "Let the Music Do the Talking," and began with a catchy guitar riff that arguably sounded more Aerosmith-like than any of Aerosmith's own songs on *Night in the Ruts*. Perry and the rest of his new band—which consisted of singer Ralph Morman, bassist David Hull, and drummer Ronnie Stewart—immediately began a tour. They did not have the drawing power of Aerosmith, of

Joe Perry went solo in early 1979.

course, and played smaller clubs, mixing original songs with covers, and even some Aerosmith tunes. The latter—and the fact that Perry had left the band in the first place—angered the remaining members of Aerosmith, especially Tyler. Soon the dejected, depressed, and drugged-out lead singer moved into the lower-class Gorham Hotel in New York City. It appeared that using heroin had become more important to him than playing music. He was also still using alcohol and other drugs. In 1980, Tyler nearly lost his life because of them.

Driving his motorcycle while high, Tyler crashed. He nearly died, and he ended up in the hospital for six months. Many thought the horrible accident—combined with Perry's leaving the band—would add up to one big lesson for Tyler. It did not. Tyler said, "I was just happy to have morphine pumped into me night and day! And then later I'd use the whole thing to get more drugs."[5]

Their Greatest Hits

Ironically, the best-selling Aerosmith album of all time was released during this period. It was called *Greatest Hits*, and was just that. It contained all the classic Aerosmith songs, including "Dream On," "Walk This Way," "Sweet Emotion," and even the band's cover of "Come Together." The album was intended to keep the Aerosmith train rolling along, even as it was falling off the tracks.

The success of *Greatest Hits* was not enough to keep guitarist Whitford from jumping off the train. He teamed up with Ted Nugent's former singer, Derek St. Holmes. The duo and two other musicians became known as Whitford/St. Holmes, and released a self-titled album in 1981. Whitford, frustrated by the direction Aerosmith was—or was not—going, decided to quit the band and tour with his new group. Rick Dufay replaced him, and the latest version of Aerosmith headed into the studio, this time in Miami, Florida. Tyler's injuries from the motorcycle accident had healed, but his drug use had not stopped. As it had been during the recording sessions for *Night in the Ruts*, it was difficult for the drugged-up Tyler to write any lyrics. This time, it was because he and Dufay were partying together. So Crespo, Perry's replacement on guitar, wrote six of the album's songs. He is often given credit for holding the band together. The resulting album was 1982's *Rock in a Hard Place*. It was hardly one of Aerosmith's classics, but it did contain a couple of decent tracks. The get-tough rocker, "Lightning Strikes," for example, held up well against many of Aerosmith's earlier songs.

The band went on a U.S. tour to support its latest album, playing stadiums from Massachusetts to California. Thetour was hit-and-miss. Sometimes the shows were good. Sometimes they were horrible. It was evident to all those who either bought the band's latest album or attended a stop on the tour—Aerosmith was not the same without Perry and Whitford.

Soon, the Joe Perry Project began experiencing hardships of its own. Most importantly, the band's leader still was frequently using drugs and alcohol. Singer Morman had left Perry's band after its first album, and sales of the second album, 1982's *I've Got the Rock 'n' Rolls Again*, were so poor that Columbia Records dropped the band. In 1983, MCA Records released the group's third album, *Once a Rocker, Always a Rocker*. When that album sold even worse than its predecessor, Perry broke up the band. It was not the only breakup the guitarist would experience. After ten years of marriage and producing one son, Adrian, he and Elyssa divorced. After the divorce, Perry often could be found sleeping on his manager's couch. As was his former bandmate Tyler, Perry was hitting bottom. Separately, both men were coming to realize that what they had together—musically at least—was something special.

Back in the Saddle Again

On Valentine's Day 1984, Perry and Whitford showed up at an Aerosmith concert. Roughly one month later, Tyler and Perry spoke on the phone and talked about a reunion. Tyler said, "I made Aerosmith work and could work with any musicians and have a real good time, but it really wasn't happening. So I went and saw Joe a couple of times and talked about it, and he said that, yeah, he felt the same way."[6] After dealing with some legal issues with his record label, Perry decided it was time to get back together with his old bandmates. He rejoined Aerosmith. So did Whitford, whose own band had had even less success than Perry's. Aerosmith's most famous lineup was now back together. How long it would last, no one knew. But the chemistry between Tyler and Perry was again near magical.

Almost immediately, Aerosmith took that chemistry on the road. They called it the "Back in the Saddle" tour. The

JOE PERRY (LEFT) REUNITED WITH STEVEN TYLER AND AEROSMITH IN 1984.

tour ran through the summer of 1984. The band played all their old classics and even incorporated a version of Perry's "Let the Music Do the Talking" into the set. At times, the shows went smoothly. Other times, alcohol and drugs hurt the performances. That was evident at a July show in Springfield, Illinois. One Aerosmith biographer said Tyler had a few drinks backstage and messed with Tom Hamilton's bass pedals. Hamilton became annoyed and hit Tyler with his guitar.[7] Later in the set, a crowd member grabbed Tyler's scarf and the singer fell off the stage. The band walked out, disgusted.[8]

Armed with a new producer, Ted Templeman, and a new record label, Geffen, Aerosmith headed into Fantasy Studios in Berkeley, California, in early summer 1985. By August, the band's eighth studio album, *Done With Mirrors*, was finished. It kicked off with a remake of Perry's "Let the Music Do the Talking," followed by "My Fist Your Face." Those two songs contained all the elements of classic Aerosmith tunes of ten years earlier—including sassy lyrics and gritty guitars. But the rest of the release sounded like it had been written quickly. It had. When it was released in November, *Done With Mirrors* sold about four hundred thousand copies. Most bands would be pleased with those figures, but Aerosmith was disappointed. The band was used to having its albums go platinum. *Done With Mirrors* was roughly six hundred thousand units short of that plateau.

One reason for the decline in sales was that mainstream musical tastes had changed since the last time the classic

Aerosmith lineup had recorded together. Lighter pop music now was topping the charts. When *Done With Mirrors* was released, only one song by a hard rock band was among the top ten singles in the country. The hard rock music Aerosmith was known for still was prominent, but younger bands were carrying the torch. Hair metal bands—so named due to their members' fondness for using a lot of hairspray to make their hair "big"—ruled the niche Aerosmith used to fill. Bands such as Mötley Crüe, Ratt, Poison, and many others—most of which had been influenced by Aerosmith in one way or another—were dominating the charts. With their tight pants, stage makeup, and sexual lyrics, those bands now were out-Aerosmithing Aerosmith.

Still, there were enough Aerosmith fans left to fill arenas from coast to coast when the band came to town. Its members were getting older, but Aerosmith's live shows remained top-notch. Loyal fans still turned out in large numbers. The trouble was, the poor-selling *Done With Mirrors* did little to attract new ones. Aerosmith had lost major momentum from its heyday of just a few years earlier. Fortunately for the band, that is when Rick Rubin called.

Groundbreaking Collaboration

Rubin was a young music producer—and Aerosmith fan—and cofounder of Def Jam Recordings. At the time, he dealt mostly with hip-hop artists, though he also dabbled in the heavy metal and rock 'n' roll worlds. In 1986, hip-hop music still was a relatively new art form and had not yet reached the masses. Rubin's idea was about to change all that. Aerosmith's manager said, "[Rubin] said he had this band called Run-D.M.C. and he wanted Steven and Joe to play on a rap version of 'Walk This Way.'"[9] Run-D.M.C. was a three-member group that had been performing their own rap version of the Aerosmith classic for years.

At first, Tyler and Perry were reluctant. They finally agreed, and spent the day in a Philadelphia studio with Rubin and the three Run-D.M.C. members, Joseph "Run" Simmons, Darryl "D.M.C." McDaniels, and Jason "Jam Master Jay" Mizell. Perry played his version of the song on guitar. Steven sang his lyrics. Run-D.M.C. rapped their version of the song, which included the use of turntables. And Rubin recorded it all.

Tyler, Perry, and the three Run-D.M.C. members soon filmed a music video for the song. The video featured Tyler and Perry on one side of a wall and the guys from Run-D.M.C. on the other side. The sides battled with each other, each one playing its version of the song before being interrupted by the other. In a symbolic ending, the two sides come together to finish the song before a large audience.

When the new version of "Walk This Way" was released in May on Run-D.M.C.'s *Raising Hell* album, both bands benefited. The song proved to be Run-D.M.C.'s breakout hit,

RUN-D.M.C. RECORDED "WALK THIS WAY" WITH AEROSMITH IN 1986.

and helped their album sell millions of copies. The song put Aerosmith back near the top of the charts. It exposed both bands to new audiences they normally would not have appealed to. The song was a crossover hit, peaking at number four on *Billboard*'s Hot 100 singles chart and at number eight on the Hot R&B/Hip-Hop Singles and Tracks singles chart. It even cracked the Top 10 on the dance charts. The first time around, "Walk This Way" helped establish Aerosmith. The second time around, it helped reestablish the band. Many believe the remake of "Walk This Way" helped save Aerosmith's career.

The music was once again doing fine, but the individual members still were not. The five men had vowed to stay sober, but when the tour began, they went back to their old ways of drinking alcohol and taking drugs. Tyler was especially out of control. The other four band members approached him about it, and the singer agreed to spend a month in a substance abuse program. There, he was told that he would quickly lapse back into his old ways if he sobered up but the other four members of Aerosmith did not. So the whole band checked into the Caron Foundation, an addiction treatment facility in Pennsylvania. Everyone involved with the band hoped the treatment would work. If it did not, it likely meant the end of Aerosmith.

BACK ON TOP

In the spring of 1987, the five members of Aerosmith entered Little Mountain Studios in Vancouver, Canada, to record their next album, *Permanent Vacation*. The recording process this time was far different than it had been for Aerosmith's previous albums. First, there was another new producer, Bruce Fairbairn, who had produced hit records for Canadian rock band Loverboy, and, most recently, the multiplatinum hit *Slippery When Wet*, for New Jersey rockers Bon Jovi. Second, the majority of the band was clean and sober for the first time. Tom Hamilton was still smoking marijuana and Joey Kramer was drinking alcohol, but the madness and unpredictability associated with the use of hardcore drugs was gone. Band members were showing up to the studio on time and, for the most part, ready to work.

The biggest change this time around was that for the first time the band was receiving help writing its songs from outside sources. Geffen A&R representative John Kalodner had insisted on it. Desmond Child, Holly Knight, and Jim Vallance were the songwriters who were brought in to work with Aerosmith. Collectively, the three writers had impressive résumés, having worked on hit songs by Bryan Adams, Bon Jovi, KISS, and many more extremely successful artists.

Band members showed some resistance to the outside help, but agreed to the new arrangements. The team immediately went to work. Vallance said, "It was literally a matter of sitting in a room with Steven and Joe, eight or ten hours at a stretch, working on songs for the album. I knew in advance they weren't happy about having to work with outside writers. I was prepared for some hostility, but it never came. We wrote most of 'Rag Doll' on the first day, and that really broke the ice and instilled confidence. They were stoked to come back the next day and continue writing."[1]

Hiring the songwriters turned out to be an excellent move. The hired hands helped write seven of the album's eleven original songs, including Top 20 hits "Dude (Looks Like a Lady)," the power ballad "Angel," and "Rag Doll." Vallance offered some insight into how "Rag Doll" was written. He said, "Joe had a riff, a really good riff . . . but it didn't go anywhere. It was just two bars that repeated. I turned it into an eight-bar phrase by introducing some underlying bass movement. . . . With that small change the verse was almost fully formed. Plus, Joe's riff was very melodic, and Steven picked up on that, vocally. The song just grew from there."[2]

Permanent Vacation was released in August 1987, and was an immediate smash. Its release had been perfectly timed to ride the momentum created by the hit remake of "Walk This Way." Aerosmith was back on top. With their newfound sobriety and new outlooks on life, it appeared they were there to stay.

The band took to the road to promote its new album, playing venues across the United States and Canada with the big names of the day, including Dokken, White Lion, and Guns N' Roses. Aerosmith even returned to Japan, where they had canceled several shows a decade earlier because of their reckless behavior. This time, they played a handful of successful gigs. *Permanent Vacation* spent sixty-seven weeks on the *Billboard* album charts. The band's fears that its fans would not like the newer, more commercial Aerosmith material were unwarranted. The album still was on the charts when Aerosmith performed "Dude (Looks Like a Lady)" at MTV's Video Music Awards ceremony in September 1988.

Personal Lives

The lives of individual band members had changed a lot by the time the *Permanent Vacation* tour came around. In November 1987, Tyler and his wife, Cyrinda Foxe, had divorced. Six months later, Tyler married costume designer Teresa Barrick. The couple had a daughter, Chelsea Anna, in 1989, then a son, Taj, in 1991.

Like Tyler, Perry also had his share of domestic changes. He married his second wife, Billie Paulette Montgomery, in the fall of 1985. She had a son, Aaron, from a previous marriage, as did Perry. After a year of marriage, another son, Tony, was born to the couple. And in 1991, the birth of son Roman rounded out the Perry family.

The other band members also had their share of domesticity. They were all married, and Tom and Terry Hamilton had even managed to stay together through all the ups and downs their life as an Aerosmith couple had dealt them. The band members were all now in their forties, and had outgrown most of the crazy ways of their youth. Aerosmith was more popular—and richer—than ever.

Because *Permanent Vacation* had been such a hit, Aerosmith decided to make very few changes for its follow-up album. In 1989, they returned to Little Mountain Studios to record. At that time, *Permanent Vacation* had just left the charts. Most of the same players were in the studio. Producer Fairbairn and songwriters Child and Vallance were back.

Hamilton finally had conquered his alcohol problem and now was sober. The team that had continued the resurrection of Aerosmith's career was ready for another round. It was a calculated move. Vallance said, "The big difference was, on *Permanent Vacation* the band were more or less forced to work with me. On *Pump*, they actually *asked* to work with me."[3]

The band was wise to do so. Musically, *Pump* picked up where *Permanent Vacation* had left off. The album still was commercial and listener-friendly. But there was more of the harder-edge sound that Aerosmith had exhibited in its early days. The opener, "Young Lust," is a throwback rocker reminiscent of many of Aerosmith's early songs. Some have said the song was meant to prove the band could still rock, and show fans that they had not sold out by using songwriters and polishing their sound to make it more radio-friendly. But Aerosmith had a history of starting their albums off with energetic songs. Even Vallance said the band was not trying to prove anything. He said, "It was nothing like that. There was no negativity behind 'Young Lust' at all. It was just me and Joe in my studio one day, and he said, 'Let's write the most rockin' track ever.' So we went for an up-tempo feel and we started jamming on a riff, and it came together very quickly. Steven arrived a few hours later. He heard our track and started improvising a melody. No lyrics, just doo-bee-doo-dah-dah. That's how he likes to work. The occasional 'keeper' phrase might pop up, but mostly he'll get a melody going and figure out the lyrics later."[4]

After "Young Lust," the album takes several twists and turns, incorporating many instruments—such as horns—not traditionally used on hard rock records. There were musical interludes between several of the songs to tie them together. As they had on *Permanent Vacation*, the song lyrics on *Pump* included traditional Aerosmith themes and subject matter. "Love in an Elevator" was sexually suggestive. "What It Takes" was a heartbreaking power ballad. "Janie's Got a Gun" was the most political song the band ever had written. The song's lyrics revolved around a woman named Janie who shot her father because he had sexually abused her. Videos from the band's songs received repeated airplay on MTV. "Janie's Got a Gun" won two of the network's Video Music Awards. That video, featuring actress Lesley Anne Warren as Janie's mother, was groundbreaking and graphic. The song also won a Grammy Award in 1991 for Best Rock Performance by a Duo or Group With Vocal. "The Other Side" won Aerosmith a third Video Music Award the following year. As did many Aerosmith songs, "The Other Side" had an interesting origin. Its songwriter said it was "written long-distance. I came up with the music and I mailed a cassette tape to Steven in Boston. He recorded his voice over my track and mailed it back to me. We finished the song over the phone."[5]

The *Pump* tour lasted a year and hit most major American

stadiums. Popular acts of the day, such as Skid Row, Joan Jett, and the Black Crowes, were openers. Aerosmith performed on *Saturday Night Live*, making a guest appearance in a popular skit with Dana Carvey and Mike Myers called "Wayne's World." The theme of that skit soon became a popular Hollywood film of the same name.

Aerosmith recorded an *MTV Unplugged* episode, performed at Monsters of Rock festivals in the United Kingdom, Italy, France, and Germany, and played at the MTV Video Music Awards. Aerosmith again returned to Japan, and then to Australia, where "Janie's Got a Gun" had been a No. 1 single. Accolades for the band continued to roll in. *Pump* sold more than four million copies. Readers of *Rolling Stone* magazine named Aerosmith the best band in America.

Video Stars

Aerosmith's next studio album, *Get a Grip*, was released in April 1993. All five band members were either in or nearing their mid-forties, but they had not lost a beat. Child and Vallance, along with a couple other songwriters, again contributed. So did producer Fairbairn. *Get a Grip* picked up where *Pump* had left off, featuring several radio-friendly songs and MTV-friendly videos. Those videos were perhaps the biggest key to Aerosmith's continued popularity. Three of them—"Cryin'," "Amazing," and "Crazy"—starred teenager Alicia Silverstone, who soon became a household name for her roles

Aerosmith performed in the skit "Wayne's World" on _Saturday Night Live_. Actor Mike Myers is at left.

in the videos and also in hit movies, such as *The Crush*, *Clueless*, and *Batman and Robin*.

The "Crazy" video also introduced Tyler's daughter Liv to the world. The two had an interesting history. Liv was born to model Bebe Buell on July 1, 1977. Tyler had a brief relationship with the model shortly before Liv was born. For years, Buell told Liv that her father was musician Todd Rundgren, the man Buell was dating at the time of Liv's birth. Buell often has said she did not want to tell Liv who her father really was because Tyler was so messed up on drugs that she felt he would be an unsuitable parent.[6]

But by 1986, the truth began coming out. Rundgren was playing in a concert in Boston and Liv was there. Steven Tyler was, too. Steven and Liv spent some time together, but Buell did not tell her Steven was her father. Two years later, Liv and her mother went into Steven's dressing room before an Aerosmith show in Mansfield, Massachusetts. When eleven-year-old Liv met nine-year-old Mia Tyler, her half-sister, she examined the girl closely. Halfway through Aerosmith's show, Liv asked her mother a question. She said, "Mom—that's my *father*, isn't it?"[7] Her mother told her it was. After the show, she told Steven that Liv knew he was her father. Steven said later that he had wanted to tell Liv he was her father for a long time.[8] A couple of years later, Liv changed her last name to Tyler. The name change—and the spot in the "Crazy" video—helped open some doors for Liv, who was doing some

Steven Tyler and his two daughters, Liv (left) and Mia (center).

modeling work. Soon, she began acting and has since starred in some popular movies, including *The Lord of the Rings*, *The Incredible Hulk*, and *Armageddon*. Aerosmith contributed four songs to the *Armageddon* sound track. One of those, "I Don't Want to Miss a Thing," was nominated for an Academy Award in 1999 for Best Song. It also was Aerosmith's first-ever No. 1 single. Award-winning songwriter Diane Warren wrote it. Some of Warren's other works include the smash hits "Because You Loved Me" by Céline Dion and "How Do I Live" by country music artists Trisha Yearwood and LeAnn Rimes.

The *Get a Grip* tour again found Aerosmith performing across the globe. It lasted through the end of 1994, and featured some high-profile stops along the way. Most noteworthy was the band's performance at the Grammy Awards ceremony in March 1994. There, they played "Livin' on the Edge," which had won the Grammy for Best Rock Performance By a Duo or Group With Vocal. "Crazy" won the same award the following year.

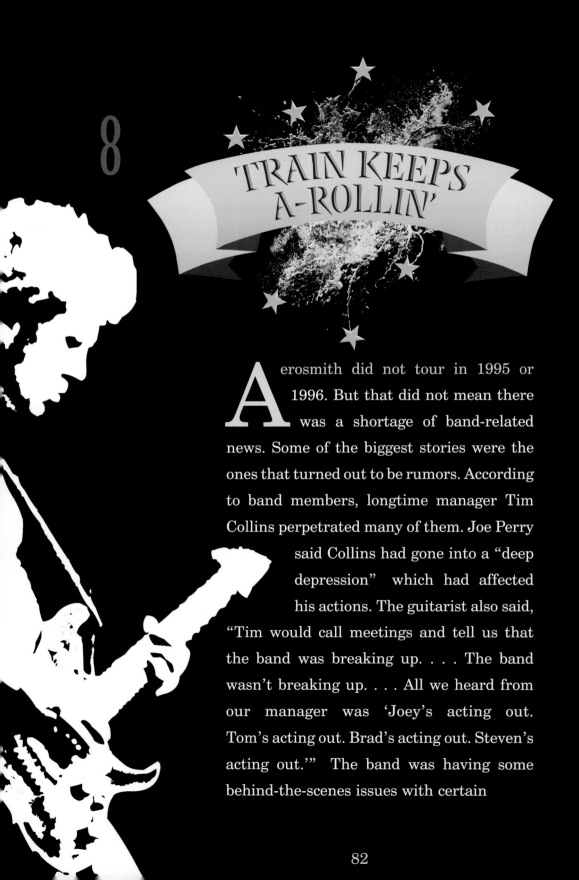

8

'TRAIN KEEPS A-ROLLIN'

Aerosmith did not tour in 1995 or 1996. But that did not mean there was a shortage of band-related news. Some of the biggest stories were the ones that turned out to be rumors. According to band members, longtime manager Tim Collins perpetrated many of them. Joe Perry said Collins had gone into a "deep depression" which had affected his actions. The guitarist also said, "Tim would call meetings and tell us that the band was breaking up. . . . The band wasn't breaking up. . . . All we heard from our manager was 'Joey's acting out. Tom's acting out. Brad's acting out. Steven's acting out.'" The band was having some behind-the-scenes issues with certain members. But they were nowhere near breaking up. Soon, Collins was fired. Aerosmith also changed record labels, leaving Geffen and re-signing with Columbia, the label that had given them their first break nearly twenty years earlier.

Several songwriters were brought in to help write material for a new Aerosmith record. This time, the extra help did more work than it had in the past. When Aerosmith's twelfth studio album, *Nine Lives*, was released in 1997, all thirteen of its songs had been at least partially written by someone who was not in the band. Many critics and fans panned the album, but many loved it. The album quickly went platinum and the song "Pink" won the band another Grammy award. "Falling in Love (Is Hard on the Knees)" won the band another Video Music Award from MTV. During the *Nine Lives* tour, the band recorded several songs for the two-disc live album, *A Little South of Sanity*, released in 1998. The album featured versions of twenty-three of Aerosmith's most popular songs, including "Dream On," "Walk This Way," and "Amazing."

Several stops on the tour were either postponed or canceled after Tyler injured his knee during a show in Anchorage, Alaska. The injury did not stop the singer—and the rest of Aerosmith—from performing at the Kennedy Space Center in Florida on June 29, 1998, during the lavish world premier party for the movie *Armageddon*, which starred Tyler's daughter Liv. The proud father was in a leg brace for the performance, but he made it through anyway. After he recovered from his injury, the band hit the road again, touring until January 1999. The band took a couple of months off, then hit the road again until July. Aerosmith took most of 2000 off from touring, but did play four sold-out shows in Japan. In January 2001, Aerosmith reemerged for two high-profile shows: one at the American Music Awards in Los Angeles, and one at the Super Bowl in Tampa, Florida, where they performed—many might say *outperformed*—with much younger chart-toppers Britney Spears, 'N Sync, Mary J. Blige, and Nelly. On March 17, the band was back in New York City to perform on *Saturday Night Live*. Two days later, Aerosmith was inducted into the Rock and Roll Hall of Fame. Michael Jackson, Queen, Paul Simon, Steely Dan, and others were inducted that same night. Each of those artists had their own hardships and issues to overcome throughout the years.

Albums Thirteen and Fourteen

Earlier that month, Aerosmith had released its latest album, *Just Push Play*. Album number thirteen did not achieve the same level of success as earlier Aerosmith albums. The band's super-successful albums, such as *Toys in the Attic*, *Rocks*, and *Pump*, set the bar so high that it would be impossible for anyone to consistently leap over. But *Just Push Play* did contain many stellar songs, including "Jaded," which reached number one on *Billboard*'s Mainstream Rock chart. *Just Push Play* went platinum a month after it was released. By Aerosmith

Aerosmith performed during halftime at Super Bowl XXXV in 2001.

standards, it was a decent seller. By a majority of bands' standards, the sales numbers were phenomenal. The *Just Push Play* tour brought people out in droves. The band even played several shows with the group that had helped spur their comeback in 1984, Run-D.M.C. Rapper-singer Kid Rock—who had given Aerosmith's Hall of Fame induction speech—also performed on that tour. In October 2003, Aerosmith even paired up with fellow 1970s heavyweights KISS on a five-month tour of the United States.

Just Push Play earned Aerosmith four Grammy nominations. The band's next studio album came in 2004. Producer Jack Douglas was back on board for the album, *Honkin' on Bobo*, and it sounds a lot like the previous hit albums they had recorded with him. "The Grind" is the only original Aerosmith song on the disc. The rest are covers the band picked to showcase the earlier blues artists that influenced them. The album cover featured a harmonica with the Aerosmith logo engraved into the top of it. *Honkin' on Bobo* peaked at number five on the *Billboard* album charts and one single, "Baby, Please Don't Go," rose to number seven on *Billboard*'s Mainstream Rock charts.

Health Problems

Aerosmith toured on the blues album until August, took some time off, then toured again from October 2005 to March 2006. That is when a scary thing happened. Tyler had to undergo throat surgery for an ailment that had bothered him off and on for years. Rumors began to circulate that the singer had throat cancer, but he did not. Resilient as ever, Tyler and the band went back on tour in September. Shortly after the jaunt began, however, Tyler did reveal that he had been diagnosed with the often-deadly liver disease hepatitis C. No one knows how Tyler got the disease, but drug users often spread it through the sharing of needles. Tyler had several months of treatment. He said, "I've had hepatitis C for a long time, asymptomatic. And I talked to my doctor . . . and he said now is the time and it's eleven months of chemotherapy. So I went on that and it about killed me."[3]

Tyler was not the only Aerosmith member to battle a potentially deadly illness. In 2006, bassist Tom Hamilton was diagnosed with throat cancer. He had several weeks of radiation therapy, and had to miss part of the band's tour. But he was back at full strength when Aerosmith embarked on a seven-month-long tour of the world in 2007. By that time, Tyler and wife Teresa Barrick had divorced, and the lead singer was dating a younger woman named Erin Brady.

Tyler turned sixty years old in 2008, with his bandmates only a few years behind. Their rock 'n' roll band has been around for nearly four decades, and has sold more than 65 million albums in the United States and more than 150 million worldwide. At ages where most musicians have long since slowed down, the members of Aerosmith keep going strong.

Former Aerosmith songwriter Jim Vallance said the band's talent is what allows them to continue to succeed. He said, "Millions of people play golf, but there's only one Tiger Woods. How many people sing or play guitar—or think they can—and yet there's only one Aerosmith. If you've ever seen them perform live or in the studio, then you have a sense of just how amazing they are. Very few bands have that ability . . . they're truly a gifted group of musicians."[4]

And successes keep coming, too. In 2004, *Rolling Stone* magazine named Aerosmith the fifty-seventh best band of all time. The magazine also listed two of the band's records, *Rocks* and *Toys in the Attic*, among its five hundred best albums of all time. Countless other "all-time best" lists include Aerosmith's songs and albums. Perry has become a guitar icon, and any best-of list involving that instrument will most likely include him.

In May 2008, Tyler entered a drug rehabilitation facility in California. Rumors began to fly that the singer had ended his longtime sobriety and had once again fallen victim to drug use. Tyler said he entered the facility to recover from foot surgeries he had to correct problems that had been caused by years of jumping around and doing acrobatics on stage. He said, "I really needed a safe environment to recuperate where I could shut off my phone and get back on my feet."[5] But one month later, Tyler admitted he had checked into the facility to overcome his addiction to pain and sleep medicines he took to recover from the surgeries

In the summer of 2008, Aerosmith became the first musical group to have an entire version of the popular *Guitar Hero* video game devoted to them. *Guitar Hero: Aerosmith* features several levels, beginning with the first show the band ever played at Nipmuc Regional High School in the fall of 1970. Much like the remake of "Walk This Way" with Run-D.M.C. did years earlier, the *Guitar Hero* game has helped expose Aerosmith to a new generation of fans. It also helped make them a lot of money. The video game manufacturer said Aerosmith earned more royalty money from *Guitar Hero: Aerosmith* than they did from any of their albums.

Tyler agreed to write an autobiography, scheduled to be published in 2010. He said, "I have so many outrageous stories, too many, and I'm gonna tell 'em all. All the unexpurgated, brain-jangling tales of debauchery, sex and drugs, transcendence and chemical dependence you will ever want to hear."[6] The book most likely will not be the last the world hears of Aerosmith. The band is one of the few that has survived the test of time—nearly forty years and counting. Band members have said more tours are likely, and new music is, too. If Aerosmith releases a new studio album, it will be their fifteenth.

Even the multiple injuries he suffered after falling from the stage during a show in August 2009 in South Dakota,

In 2008, the video game *Guitar Hero: Aerosmith* was released.
From left to right: Joey Kramer, Steven Tyler, Joe Perry (playing
the game), Brad Whitford, and Tom Hamilton.

could not stop Tyler. He said, "People ask us, 'How long are you going to keep doing it?' What kind of real answer is there for that? Until my face is ripping off of my skull. Then I won't do it. Believe me, when I look up and go, 'Uh, Joe, we're really looking old,' then I'll say let's get the [heck] out of here while we can."[7]

TIMELINE

1948—Steven Tyler (Steven Victor Tallarico) is born March 26 in Yonkers, New York.

1950—Joey Kramer is born June 21 in the Bronx, New York; Anthony Joseph "Joe" Perry is born September 10 in Lawrence, Massachusetts.

1951—Tom Hamilton is born December 31 in Colorado Springs, Colorado.

1952—Brad Whitford is born February 23 in Winchester, Massachusetts.

1970—Aerosmith plays their first show at Nipmuc Regional High School in Mendon, Massachusetts.

1972—Aerosmith signs a $125,000 contract with Columbia Records.

1973—Aerosmith releases their first album, *Aerosmith*; they perform "Dream On" on the TV show *American Bandstand*.

1974—*Get Your Wings* is released; Aerosmith appears on the TV show *Midnight Special*.

1975—*Toys in the Attic* is released.

1976—"Dream On" is rereleased and becomes a Top 10 single; *Rocks* is released.

1977—*Draw the Line* is released.

1978—Aerosmith appears in *Sgt. Pepper's Lonely Hearts Club Band* film, and they remake the Beatles' song "Come Together."

1979—*Night in the Ruts* is released; Joe Perry leaves Aerosmith to begin the Joe Perry Project; Perry is replaced by Jimmy Crespo.

1980—*Aerosmith's Greatest Hits* is released.

1981—Brad Whitford leaves Aerosmith and is replaced by Rick Dufay.

1982—*Rock in a Hard Place* is released.

1984—Joe Perry and Brad Whitford rejoin Aerosmith.

1985—*Done With Mirrors* is released on Geffen Records.

1986—Rap group Run-D.M.C. covers the Aerosmith song "Walk This Way," with the participation of Joe Perry and Steven Tyler; the entire band enters a drug treatment facility.

1987—*Permanent Vacation* is released, which includes "Dude (Looks Like a Lady)," Aerosmith's first Top 40 hit in nine years.

1989—*Pump* is released.

1990—"Janie's Got a Gun" wins the MTV Video Music Awards for Best Heavy Metal/Hard Rock Video and Viewer's Choice; the band performs on *Saturday Night Live.*

1991—"Janie's Got a Gun" wins the Grammy Award for Best Rock Vocal Performance by a Duo or Group; Aerosmith re-signs to Columbia Records; the band releases a box set, *Pandora's Box.*

1993—*Get a Grip* is released; the band performs on *Saturday Night Live*; "Livin' on the Edge" wins the MTV Video Music Award for Viewer's Choice.

1994—"Livin' on the Edge" wins the Grammy Award for Best Rock Vocal Performance by a Duo or Group; "Cryin'" wins the MTV Video Music Awards for Video of the Year, Best Group Video, and Viewer's Choice

1995—"Crazy" wins the Grammy Award for Best Rock Vocal Performance by a Duo or Group.

1997—*Nine Lives* is released; "Falling in Love (Is Hard on the Knees)" wins the MTV Video Music Award for Best Rock Video.

95

1998—"I Don't Want to Miss a Thing" from the sound track to the movie *Armageddon* becomes Aerosmith's first No. 1 single; the band wins the MTV Video Music Awards for "I Don't Want to Miss a Thing" (Best Video From a Film) and "Pink" (Best Rock Video).

1999—"Pink" wins the Grammy Award for Best Rock Vocal Performance by a Duo or Group.

2001—Aerosmith performs at the halftime show of Super Bowl XXXV; *Just Push Play* is released; Aerosmith is inducted into the Rock and Roll Hall of Fame; "Jaded" becomes a No. 1 single.

2004—*Honkin' on Bobo* is released

2006—Steven Tyler reveals his battle with hepatitis C; Tom Hamilton is treated for throat cancer.

2008—Steven Tyler enters a drug rehabilitation center; *Guitar Hero: Aerosmith* is released.

2009—Steven Tyler suffers multiple injuries after he falls off the stage during a show in South Dakota.

DISCOGRAPHY

1973—*Aerosmith*

1974—*Get Your Wings*

1975—*Toys in the Attic*

1976—*Rocks*

1977—*Draw the Line*

1978—*Live! Bootleg*

1979—*Night in the Ruts*

1980—*Greatest Hits*

1982—*Rock in a Hard Place*

1985—*Done With Mirrors*

1986—*Classics Live!*

1987—*Permanent Vacation*

      Classics Live! II

1988—*Gems*

1989—*Pump*

1991—*Pandora's Box*

1993—*Get a Grip*

1994—*Big Ones*

      Box of Fire

1997—*Nine Lives*

1998—*A Little South of Sanity*

2001—*Just Push Play*

Young Lust: The Aerosmith Anthology—The Geffen Years

2002—*O, Yeah! Ultimate Aerosmith Hits*

2004—*Honkin' on Bobo*

2005—*Rockin' the Joint*

2006—*Devil's Got a New Disguise: The Very Best of Aerosmith*

CONCERT TOURS

1973—Opening for Mott the Hoople

1974—Opening for Uriah Heep and Blue Öyster Cult

1975—*Toys in the Attic* Tour

1976–1977—*Rocks* Tour

1977–1978—Aerosmith Express Tour

1978–1979—*Live! Bootleg* Tour

1979–1980—*Night in the Ruts* Tour

1982–1984—*Rock in a Hard Place* Tour

1984—Back in the Saddle Tour

1985–1986—*Done With Mirrors* Tour

1987–1988—*Permanent Vacation* Tour

1989–1990—*Pump* Tour

1993–1994—*Get a Grip* Tour

1997–1999—*Nine Lives* Tour

2001—*Just Push Play* Tour

2002—Girls of Summer Tour

2003—Aerosmith/KISS Tour

2004—*Honkin' on Bobo* Tour

2005–2006—Rockin' the Joint Tour

2006—Route of All Evil Tour

2007—World Tour 2007

GLOSSARY

45—A type of vinyl musical record, usually containing one song on each side. So named because it spins on a player at 45 revolutions per minute.

bar—A segment of music.

Billboard—A magazine devoted to the music industry.

cover—A new version of a previously recorded song.

debauchery—Overindulgence of sensual pleasures.

entourage—A group of people traveling with someone to provide assistance or friendship, generally for an important person.

flamboyant—Ornate, showy, or brilliant.

gold album—A music album that has sold a minimum of five hundred thousand copies.

Grammy—An annual honor given by the Recording Academy for outstanding achievements in the recording industry; the musical equivalent of an Academy Award.

heavy metal—A style of music that features loud guitars, soaring vocals, and pounding drums.

hepatitis C—An often deadly viral infection of the liver that can be spread through the sharing of needles by drug users.

heroin—An addictive narcotic drug, illegal in the United States and many other countries; derived from the opium poppy plant.

hip-hop—A form of popular music closely related to rap.

marquee—A large sign often located above the entrance to a theater.

platinum album—A music album having sold a minimum of one million copies.

pop music—Any genre of music that is commercial friendly and marketable, often featuring memorable lyrics and music.

record label—A company, or branch of a company, that produces and promotes musical offerings.

record producer—A person who oversees the making of a record.

royalty—A share of the profits made from a recording or other piece of work.

sound track—The music from a motion picture, often released for commercial purposes.

suburb—A small community located outside of a large city or town.

synagogue—A Jewish house of worship.

CHAPTER NOTES

Chapter 1. Sweet Emotion

1. Nekesa Mumbi Moody, "Rock and Roll Hall of Fame Entries," Associated Press, reproduced at *Rock This Way*, n.d., <http://www.rockthisway.de/news/news_march01.htm> (April 13, 2008).

2. Robert Mancini, "Aerosmith Thrilled, Steely Dan Unimpressed at Rock Hall Ceremony," *MTV.com*, March 20, 2001, <http://www.mtv.com/news/articles/1441929/20010320/aerosmith.jhtml> (April 13, 2008).

3. Bruce Simon, "Aerosmith In-Store Brings Out Hordes of Loyal Fans," *Yahoo! Music*, March 19, 2001, <http://music.yahoo.com/read/news/12062989> (April 13, 2008).

4. "Mom Rocks," *New York Observer*, March 25, 2001, <http://www.observer.com/node/44177> (April 20, 2008).

5. Darren Davis, "Aerosmith Thankful to be in Rock Hall," *Yahoo! Music*, March 21, 2001, <http://music.yahoo.com/read/news/12032042> (April 10, 2008).

6. Ibid.

Chapter 2. Coming Together

1. Aerosmith with Stephen Davis, *Walk This Way:*

The Autobiography of Aerosmith (New York: HarperEntertainment, 1997), p. 20.

2. Ibid., p. 20

3. Ibid., p. 24

4. Ibid.

5. Phil Alexander, "The Mojo Interview," *Mojo*, May 2007, <http://www.hessentag2007.de/fileadmin/ 1.6Downloadmaterial/aero_mojo_interview.pdf> (July 3, 2008).

6. Aerosmith with Stephen Davis, p. 27.

7. Ibid., p. 41.

8. Scott Cohen, "The Circus Magazine Interview: Aerosmith's Steven Tyler," reproduced at *AeroForceOne.com*, n.d., <http://forums.aeroforceone. com/viewtopic.php?t=57313&postdays=0&postorder= asc&start=60&sid=ca03b19c4f9f9e0cb0c1c3a3e72 e8ff3> (July 8, 2008).

9. Ibid.

10. Aerosmith with Stephen Davis, p. 31.

11. Ibid., p. 32.

12. Ibid., p. 61.

13. Ibid., p. 60.

14. Ibid., p. 62.

15. "Joey Kramer" biography, *AeroForceOne.com*, n.d., <http://www.aeroforceone.com/index.cfm/pk/ content/pid/1015844> (July 5, 2008).

Chapter 3. Ragged Start

1. Paul Crocetti, "New 'Guitar Hero' to Feature Site

of Aerosmith's First Show," *Weston Town Crier*, April 23, 2008, <http://www.wickedlocal.com/weston/archive/x914615273> (July 12, 2008).

2. Aerosmith with Stephen Davis, *Walk This Way: The Autobiography of Aerosmith* (New York: HarperEntertainment, 1997), p. 109.

3. Scott Cohen, "The *Circus* Magazine Interview: Aerosmith's Steven Tyler," reproduced at *AeroForceOne.com*, n.d. <http://forums.aeroforceone.com/viewtopic.php?t=57313&postdays=0&postorder=asc&start=60&sid=ca03b19c4f9f9e0cb0c1c3a3e72e8ff3> (July 12, 2008).

4. Martin Huxley, *Aerosmith: The Fall and the Rise of Rock's Greatest Bands* (New York: St. Martin's Press, 1995), p. 18.

5. Aerosmith with Stephen Davis, p. 121.

6. Ibid., p. 130.

7. Ibid., p. 141.

8. Mark Putterford, *The Fall and Rise of Aerosmith* (London: Omnibus Press, 1991), p. 15.

Chapter 4. "Dream On"

1. Aerosmith with Stephen Davis, *Walk This Way: The Autobiography of Aerosmith* (New York: HarperEntertainment, 1997), p. 168.

2. Mark Putterford, *The Fall and Rise of Aerosmith* (London: Omnibus Press, 1991), p. 17.

3. Ken Sharp, "Weathering the Storms," *Goldmine*, April 4, 2007, reproduced at *AeroForceOne.com*,

n.d., <http://www.aeroforceone.com/index.cfm/pk/
view/cd/Naa/cdid/850785/pid/302766> (August 13,
2008).

4. "Looking Back: Aerosmith—Classic Rock,"
   AeroForceOne.com, May 16, 2006, <https://www.
   aeroforceone.com/index.cfm/pk/view/cd/naa/cdid/
   648316/pid/302766> (February 17, 2009).

5. Martin Power, *The Complete Guide to the Music of
   Aerosmith* (London: Omnibus Press, 1997), p. 3.

6. "Movies and Specials: American Bandstand's
   50th . . . A Celebration," *AllYourTV.com*, n.d.,
   <http://www.allyourtv.com/moviesspecials/a/
   moviesspecialsamericanbandstands50th.html>
   (August 22, 2008).

7. Martin Huxley, *Aerosmith: The Fall and the Rise
   of Rock's Greatest Bands* (New York: St. Martin's
   Press, 1995), p. 35.

8. Aerosmith with Stephen Davis, p. 223.

9. Ibid.

10. Putterford, p. 24.

11. Phil Alexander, "The *Mojo* Interview," *Mojo*, May
    2007, <http://www.hessentag2007.de/fileadmin/
    1.6Downloadmaterial/aero_mojo_interview.pdf>
    (July 3, 2008).

Chapter 5. Falling Apart

1. Martin Huxley, *Aerosmith: The Fall and the Rise
   of Rock's Greatest Bands* (New York: St. Martin's
   Press, 1995), p. 49.

2. Mark Putterford, *The Fall and Rise of Aerosmith* (London: Omnibus Press, 1991), p. 17.

3. Aerosmith with Stephen Davis, *Walk This Way: The Autobiography of Aerosmith* (New York: HarperEntertainment, 1997), p. 282.

4. Ibid., p. 285.

5. Putterford, p. 67.

6. Martin Power, *The Complete Guide to the Music of Aerosmith* (London: Omnibus Press, 1997), p. 39.

7. Billy Altman, "Aerosmith: *Draw the Line*," *Rolling Stone*, March 9, 1978, p. 54.

8. Johnny Angel, "Kickin' Back With Jack Douglas," *KNAC.com*, February 28, 2000, reproduced at *RateYourMusic.com*, n.d., <http://rateyourmusic. com/list/JonFox/aerosmith_a_to_z> (July 13, 2008).

9. Janet Maslin, "Son of Sgt. Pepper: Many Forms Involved," *New York Times*, July 21, 1978, p. 16.

10. Aerosmith with Stephen Davis, p. 311.

Chapter 6. Sobering Decisions

1. Aerosmith with Stephen Davis, *Walk This Way: The Autobiography of Aerosmith* (New York: HarperEntertainment, 1997), p. 300.

2. Ibid., p. 311.

3. Cyrinda Foxe-Tyler and Danny Fields, *Dream On: Livin' on the Edge with Steven Tyler and Aerosmith* (New York: Berkley Boulevard, 2000), p. 180.

4. Mark Putterford, *The Fall and Rise of Aerosmith* (London: Omnibus Press, 1991), p. 41.

5. Ibid., p. 45.

6. Martin Huxley, *Aerosmith: The Fall and the Rise of Rock's Greatest Bands* (New York: St. Martin's Press, 1995), p. 126.

7. Ibid., p. 130.

8. Ibid.

9. Aerosmith with Stephen Davis, p. 434.

Chapter 7. Back on Top

1. Personal interview with Jim Vallance, August 20, 2008.

2. Ibid.

3. Ibid.

4. Ibid.

5. Ibid.

6. Bebe Buell biography, *The Internet Movie Database*, n.d., <http://www.imdb.com/name/nm0119143/bio> (August 2, 2008).

7. Aerosmith with Stephen Davis, *Walk This Way: The Autobiography of Aerosmith* (New York: HarperEntertainment, 1997), p. 451.

8. Ibid., p. 467.

Chapter 8. Train Keeps A-Rollin'

1. Aerosmith with Stephen Davis, *Walk This Way: The Autobiography of Aerosmith* (New York: HarperEntertainment, 1997), p. 490.

2. Ibid.

3. Associated Press, "Steven Tyler Reveals Battle With Hepatitis C," reproduced at *Billboard.com*, n.d., <http://www.billboard.com/bbcom/news/article_display.jsp?vnu_content_id=1003157395> (August 23, 2008).

4. Personal interview with Jim Vallance, August 20, 2008.

5. Mike Fleeman, "Steven Tyler: I Went to Rehab for Foot Surgery," *People.com*, May 29, 2008, <http://www.people.com/people/article/0,,20203288,00.html> (August 13, 2008).

6. Associated Press, "Memoir Promising 'Brain-jangling Tales'," *(Fort Wayne, IN) Journal-Gazette*, August 8, 2008, p. W-11.

7. Isaac Guzman, "Oldies and Still Goodies: Aerosmith Has a Hit LP on Eve of Its Induction into Hall of Fame," *New York Daily News*, March 14, 2001, p. 41.

FURTHER READING

Books

Anjou, Erik. *Aerosmith*. Philadelphia, Penn.: Chelsea House, 2002.

Brasch, Nicolas. *Pop and Rock Music*. North Mankato, Minn.: Smart Apple Media, 2004.

Kenney, Karen Latchana. *Cool Rock Music: Create and Appreciate What Makes Music Great!* Edina, Minn.: ABDO Pub., 2008.

Schaefer, A.R. *Forming a Band*. Mankato, Minn.: Capstone High-Interest Books, 2004.

Internet Addresses

The Official Aerosmith Site
<http://www.aerosmith.com>

Rolling Stone: Aerosmith
<http://www.rollingstone.com/artists/aerosmith>

INDEX